Emotional Learning

SUSTAINING SUCCESS DESPITE LIFE'S UPS AND DOWNS

Jim Harris

Harris, Jim (James R.M.)

Emotional Learning:
Gaining Success & Security in a World of Change
Includes bibliographical references and index.

1. Emotions. 2. Learning.

Emotional Learning is also available on audio CD and cassette.

I would very much welcome your comments on Emotional Learning. E-mail Jim Harris at jimh@jimharris.com – and if your suggestions are incorporated in a future edition of the book, he will thank you in the acknowledgements, and send you a complimentary copy of the subsequent edition.

Editors: Michael Cormack and Victoria Musgrave
Cover Designer: Kate Anthony
Audio CD Engineering: Colin Nanton
Layout and Graphics: Leasa Paquette

Grateful acknowledgement is made for permission to reprint excerpt from the following work:

The Rabbi's Gift as it appears in M. Scott Peck's *The Different Drum* (Simon & Schuster, 1987), page 13-15 is reprinted with permission.

Printed in Canada
First Edition: September 2002
ISBN 0-9689763-5-2

What people say about Jim Harris' work:

The Learning Paradox

"*The Learning Paradox* is a rich, in depth exploration of the major issues facing today's organizations. But it's more than that – it's filled with stories and examples that evoke curiosity, laughter, and true learning. Long after I put the book down, I found myself thinking about many of the lessons Jim Harris describes so well."

Meg Wheatley, **author** *Leadership & The New Science*

"In *The Learning Paradox*, Harris offers a strikingly insightful and coherent organizational learning strategy for businesses in this rapidly changing world."

Hunter & Amory Lovins, co-authors *Natural Capitalism*, **Founders Rocky Mountain Institute**

"Syncrude is the largest oil sands operation in the world. In a technically advanced and continually evolving business such as ours, it's vitally important for our people to constantly learn, change and adapt to uncertainty. In *The Learning Paradox*, Jim Harris' message is clear, concise and powerful. In fact, I was so impressed by the book that I had Jim present its theories to our entire executive and management team."

Eric P. Newell, Chairman and CEO, Syncrude

" *The Learning Paradox* deals with the challenges of incessant change and helps make sense of the confusion, emerging trends and technologies. With profound insight, the book presents practical, proven strategies, tools, tips and techniques to individuals and organizations to thrive in today's fast changing business environment. I highly recommend you read the book – it had the same impact on me that Alvin Toffler's *Future Shock* did in 1971."

Larry Wilson, Founder of Wilson Learning & Co-author *The One Minute Sales Person* and *Stop Selling Start Partnering*

"If I were told that my people and I could read only one business book during the next year I would, in a heartbeat, choose Jim Harris' *The Learning Paradox.* I choose this book because it communicates so very clearly not only the key issues we face, but the solutions we need for survival. This book is priceless.

Lou   Pritchett,   retired   Vice-President,   Sales, Procter & Gamble

"Every day the future keeps coming at us whether we like it or not. *The Learning Paradox* provides individuals and organizations with the keys to unlock the right attitude and the mechanism for developing the necessary skills to go out and meet the future with confidence."

Kenneth Clarke, Chairman, Royal LePage

Jim Harris' Seminars

"Jim's session was one of the most highly rated and I am certain that we will work with him in the future. What was particularly noteworthy was the accessibility and relevance of his material. Jim's friendly, open style is critical in encouraging participants to take the material on board and shift their thinking."
Geoff Merchant, Centre for Management & Policy Studies, UK Cabinet Office

Blindsided!

"In the fast-paced global business environment, the possibility of being blindsided by a competitor or new market entrant is very real, even for businesses that appear most secure. Jim Harris offers real-life examples that will cause the reader to stop, think and question whether he or she is doing everything in his or her power to avoid being blindsided. A must-read for all senior executives."
Clare Hart, President & CEO of Factiva, a Dow Jones & Reuters Company

Dedicated to life long learners.

Strategic Advantage Mission Statement

We work to change the world by changing
ourselves and by helping our clients change.

Strategic Advantage is a learning and teaching organization.
We study emerging trends and technologies and their
potential impact on businesses. We are committed to
advancing the understanding and practice of
cutting-edge leadership and assisting our clients –
individuals and organizations – achieve the greatest possible
security within a dynamic and changing marketplace.

Contents

CHAPTER 2 **The Learning Paradox.** We cannot predict the future –
security for individuals and organizations is based on
the ability to learn, change and accept uncertainty.
Paradoxically this is what we fear most. 41

CHAPTER 3 **Leadership.** Management focuses on
problem solving; leadership focuses on

Introduction

How this Book Began

The concept for *Emotional Learning* emerged in 2002 when I spoke at the Achievers weekend conference for the top 500 business leaders of InterBiz. J.P. Pawliw-Fry, one of only a few consultants licensed by Daniel Goleman to teach *Emotional Intelligence*, was speaking on Friday night and I was speaking the next morning. J.P.'s powerful presentation overwhelmed me –I stayed up till four in the morning thinking about how *Emotional Intelligence* supported the themes of my second book *The Learning Paradox*.

Emotional Intelligence, Daniel Goleman's bestseller, argues that emotional intelligence, which he calls "emotional quotient" or EQ, is more important than the traditional intelligence quotient (or IQ) in determining success in life and business. In other words, how we get along with other people is more important than how much we know.

The Learning Paradox, my second bestseller, argues that 80 percent of the technology we will use in our day-to-day lives in just 10 years hasn't even been invented yet. Therefore, job security today is based on learning, changing and accepting uncertainty. Paradoxically, what we fear most as adults is learning, changing and uncertainty. Our job security is based on the very thing we fear the most.

Success today is based on overcoming the emotional barriers that prevent us from living life to the fullest, and continually learning. The links between the two books were very strong in my mind.

For me *Emotional Intelligence* is best summed up by the story of the Taoist Farmer....

Chapter One

Emotional Learning

The Taoist Farmer[4]

In a poor country village, there was a farmer who was considered to be rich. He owned a horse, which he used for plowing and transportation. One day his horse ran away. The villagers said, "What terrible luck, you have lost all your wealth!" The farmer simply replied, "Maybe."

A few days later his horse came back bringing with it two wild horses. And the villagers said, "What incredible luck, you have just *tripled* your wealth!" But the farmer just said, "Maybe."

The next day the farmer's only son was out riding one of the wild horses, trying to tame it, when it bucked him off and he broke his leg (3,000 years ago that was life threatening). All the villagers said, "What terrible luck, your *only* son with a broken leg!" But the farmer just said, "Maybe."

The next week the Emperor's men came through the village conscripting every young man to fight in a war, taking every young man except for the farmer's son. The villagers said, "What *incredible* luck." And the farmer just said, "Maybe."

Sometimes what I think are the best situations in life turn out to be the worst, and sometimes the worst are the seedbed upon which magnificent things are built. I only really understand in hindsight.

The real question for me is how do I live life with the calm, joy, serenity and the maximum contribution of the farmer despite what is happening – because I really don't want my emotional life to follow the NASDAQ index!

Buddhists believe that all suffering is caused by attachment – attachment to people, places, things and outcomes of situations. When things don't go the way I want them to – like a three-year-old, I am apt to throw a temper tantrum (but in the most adult way possible). The story of the farmer helps me to understand that I have to live life on life's terms. In the Bible, there's a story in which Christ advises the reader to wear clothes loosely – meaning accept the twists and turns that life gives us. When I am not attached to an outcome, I can live life joyfully no matter what is happening. This philosophy helps me live comfortably amid a rapidly changing world.

This is called re-framing – seeing a situation in a completely different light. I use re-framing in every day life to cope with challenges. Let me give an example. Everyone knows what the fast lane is for on the highway – for people driving *fast*. When I am in the fast lane and there is someone driving slowly in front of me, rather than get upset, I think how they could be saving me a speeding ticket because perhaps there is a radar trap ahead. This then encourages me to slow down and drive more responsibly.

I admire the Taoist farmer because he accepts the challenges and unpredictability of life. He is emotionally mature, capable of living joyfully despite challenge and capable of making decisions based on his values rather than just reacting.

Emotional Intelligence

The Taoist Farmer tells the story of *Emotional Intelligence*. Daniel Goleman argues that IQ [intelligence quotient] determines only about 20 per cent of life success,[2] and instead emotional intelligence is more important. *Emotional Intelligence* is made up of:

1. *Self-awareness.* Recognizing feelings as they occur.
2. *Managing Emotions.* So you are not a slave to your emotions.
3. *Motivating Yourself.* Emotional self-control such as delaying gratification and stopping impulsiveness. Also being positive in the face of adversity.
4. *Empathy with Others.*
5. *Handling Relationships.*

There are a number of insights to be gleaned from *Emotional Intelligence*. As human beings we have the fight or flight response. When we feel threatened the adrenalin begins pumping, the heart rate accelerates, and we prepare to fight or flee. Our ability to focus increases exponentially; however, our ability to think laterally and creatively plummets dramatically.

There are anthropological reasons for this phenomenon: when our ancestors lived on the plains of Africa we needed the fight or flight response to cope with saber-toothed tigers. Today, though our physical security is rarely threatened, we still have the same response whenever we feel threatened in any way. Threaten my pride or my ego and you'll arouse the fight or flight response. In other words, emotional threats, not just physical threats, arouse the fight or flight response.

The danger, of course, is that I will react out of anger, fear or resentment rather than the values I believe in – love, compassion, tolerance and acceptance. In a highly emotional state I am apt to suffer an "amygdala hijack." The amygdala is one of the oldest parts of the brain and it's responsible for the fight or flight response.

Emotional Intelligence teaches three powerful lessons:

1. My initial reaction to any situation is based on emotion, not logic. In other words, EQ is more important than IQ.
2. When I am in full fight or flight, my creative thinking powers falls dramatically;
3. That I have to calm down when I am angry, threatened, or resentful to restore my full thinking and creative powers.

I used to represent Stephen Covey teaching *The Seven Habits of Highly Effective People* to clients. One of the central messages is that we need to separate stimulus from response. Habit one is "be proactive," that is, I need to determine my response to any situation based on my values rather than my initial reaction.

This is why it is so important to take a "time out" when I am angry or resentful so that I can calm down and avoid doing something stupid that I may later regret.

I live on a three-lane street. Cars park on one side of the street leaving two lanes for traffic. There are a lot of little children on our street and a playground, so it's a 40 km/hour (25 mph) speed zone. Occasionally, a young kid driving a souped up car will come racing down the street – and if I am driving towards him I will get a brilliant idea – "I should turn into his lane, then he'd slow down." If I actually acted on the thought would there now be one or two idiots on my street?

Another time, I was driving down my street with my wife in the passenger's seat. Someone had parked on the wrong side of the road leaving only the center lane unblocked. The laws of the road require that if a car is illegally parked on your side of the street, thereby blocking your path, you must give the right of way to drivers coming the other way. I was coming the other way but this guy decided to pull into the center lane, blocking me. I was in the right and he wasn't. And I was not about to give way. My wife just looked

at me. This guy's wife or girlfriend was in the front seat with him and just looked at him. I am sure the women couldn't believe it. We just sat there. I thought to myself, "I can stay here all day buddy. Just try me." And I was serious. I was willing to wait all day.

Finally he backed down and backed up (which was the right thing for him to do).

You know driving may be the ultimate test of spiritual development.

But was my response logical or was it emotional? The insight that we typically make decisions based on emotion not logic – is powerful.

Always Searching

I am a really bright guy – or so I think – and I like to analyze things and get to the root of an issue or problem. All my life I have been searching for something. Something has been missing. In high school I looked up to the seniors as Gods. They were really cool. I thought, "When I become a senior, *then* I will have arrived. *Then* life will really begin. *Then* I'll be happy and fulfilled."

I eagerly waited for my senior year, but when it arrived, it was not as exciting as I thought it would be. There was more freedom, but now the really "cool" place to be was university.

My first year of university was completely different, and a whole new life of independence opened up. However, something was still missing.

I thought about it a bit – and then, "Aha!" – it came to me. What I was missing was a motorcycle. If I just had a bike, then life would really begin.

So I got the bike, but no, that wasn't quite it either. After some more serious reflection I realized what I was lacking – it was a blond on my arm. If I just had a gorgeous girlfriend, then I'd be really happy. So I got the girlfriend and no, that wasn't quite it.

Then I began thinking, if I were just single again. Then things would really be happening.

And the list of things that I needed to have or do continued: getting elected as a student politician, winning a scholarship, being on a couple of university sports teams. And then after university what I felt I needed was to travel around the world. Then it was writing a book, achieving bestseller status, becoming a top-tier speaker, the list was endless.

What is Wrong with this Picture?

I've realized in hindsight that I was always looking forward to the future – and never living in the present.

Life is circular. When you talk to people in their 70s and 80s, they wish they were teenagers again!

"Familiarity breeds contempt," goes the saying. I can become familiar with any situation, material possession, relationship, etc. Far fields will always look greener.

When will I "arrive" and find contented happiness and bliss? If arriving is dependent upon external things – material possessions, relationships, my job, my title – then I am doomed to a life of insecurity and lack of fulfillment. Because no matter how much I accumulate, someone will always have more.

Be-Do-Have

Here is a very simple, powerful model:

Be ⟶ Do ⟶ Have

Now many people in Western countries don't adopt the be-do-have philosophy. Instead they live by:

Have ⟶ Do ⟶ Be

Many people think, "If I win the lottery, I will *have* a million dollars, then I will be able to *do* certain things, then I will *be* happy."

Or at work people think, "If I *have* a certain job title, then I will be able to *do* certain things, then I will *be* successful." Or people in companies believe, "If we *have* a certain market share, then we'll be able to launch certain market initiatives (*do*), then we'll *be* movers and shakers." Or in my personal life, "If I *have* a spouse or children, then we will *do* certain things as a family, then I will *be* fulfilled."

The danger with this philosophy is that my internal state of *being* (happiness, security, self-esteem and fulfilment) is a function of external circumstances (*doing* and *having*). If what I have or do is ever taken away from me – who am I?

This outside-in approach inherently creates insecurity. If my security comes from people, places or things, and circumstances change, I lose my security. If I derive my security from external factors and these are taken away from me (I don't get the promotion, I lose my job, my spouse dies or the house burns down), then I lose my security, happiness and sense of self-worth. Grieving loss is human, but using it to define our existence is dangerous. Lasting security, stability and happiness can only be a function of being – who I am and what values I believe in.

For instance, if I was an Olympic athlete and defined my sense of self-esteem by my physical prowess, and I was in a car accident and my legs were crushed, who would I be? Probably a candidate for suicide. But am I more than my legs?

In 1999, my mother-in-law, Marg, discovered she had breast cancer and underwent a radical mastectomy followed by chemotherapy. She showed tremendous courage through the whole experience and I am happy to report the cancer is in complete remission. As Marg says, "My breasts don't define me." Not even the physical body I inhabit defines who I am.

My mother-in-law's battle with breast cancer was a very difficult experience – for my wife and I, for her husband Mac and for her. How could any good have come from it? The story of the Taoist farmer suggests that something good will come out of even the most challenging situations. Marg's cancer brought us very close together as a family.

One of the most poignant moments of my life – and one of the strongest regrets I have – is when my wife and I were visiting Marg and Mac in Montreal. Marg had begun chemotherapy – but her hair hadn't fallen out yet. We were all at a hair salon that works with women who have cancer. One of the things they recommended was that Marg proactively shave her head. It's a step that lets the individual feel that they are in control and making the choices. The alternative would have been for her to wake up and find a clump of hair on the pillow, or to take a shower and have whole wads of hair fall out. Marg decided to shave her head. We were going to buy her a couple of wigs.

All of a sudden an idea struck me – I could shave my head too. It would be a beautiful statement of support for Marg. But then I realized that I was going to be speaking at a conference the following week – and knew that I would be self-conscious being bald for the first time in my life. So fear prevented me from having a beautiful experience – letting my mother-in-law know how much I love her – with or without hair, with or without breasts.

An Imaginary Trip

Come with me on an imaginary trip. I often do this visioning exercise. I imagine that I am going to the funeral of a very good friend. And there is a lot of sadness in my heart because this person was very special to me. As I arrive at the church or the synagogue, I see so many good, mutual friends – and there is a tremendous sadness in their hearts – I can tell this person was very special to them also. As I walk down the aisle there is a growing sense of unease in my heart. There is something very wrong. I arrive at the front, look down and see myself in the coffin. Like some drunk, I stagger backwards and fall into a pew.

All of a sudden I realize I am a ghost at my own funeral. My life is over. I have left this beautiful place we call earth. Now there is a deeper sadness in my heart.

I listen to four people get up and say what my life meant to them. What do I want to be remembered for?

My sister gets up and relates what I was like as a brother. What would I want her to say? That I was loving, kind and tolerant. That I always had time for her, when she needed help.

A business associate gets up and says what I was like to work with. How did I treat people who I worked with? Was I fair? Honest?

Someone from my high school or university days talks – what was I like in my formative years?

And finally someone from the community or one of my friends speaks. What would they say?

The answers I get from this exercise are very important – because they tell me how I should orient my life. The exercise draws out the values to base my life on – the values I should use to decide how to respond to situations. The exercise helps me answer question such as: How do I want to make decisions in my life? How do I want to live? What is my mission? Why am I here? What is the purpose of my life?

Being Off Course

An airplane is off course 98 percent of the time because it is constantly being blown off course by wind shifts. The pilot or the auto-pilot is always having to make slight corrections and at times even change the flight path to avoid thunderstorms. Do you think the pilot says to himself, "I am a bad, bad pilot. I have been off course 98 percent of the time. I am going to give up heading to Cincinnati and instead go to Buffalo."

Or imagine that the pilot eventually got so depressed about being off course all the time that he decided to take Prozac so that he'd be happy. His newfound happiness wouldn't improve the situation.

And it's the same way with me – I have certain values I want to live by – but I am off course an awful lot of the time. I am not as patient, compassionate, forgiving, disciplined, or courageous as I would like to be, but I try. I have a personal mission statement, and I work to create a vision of the kind of future that I would like to experience. Just because I am off course frequently, doesn't mean that I should give up the destination.

An Equally Powerful Question

An equally powerful question is to ask, what do I not want to be remembered for? Imagine someone saying, "What I will always remember about Jim was the metallic blue tint of his BMW. You know I loved the color of his car."

Or, "What will linger always in my mind was the scent of his cologne. I think it was Polo by Ralph Lauren."

Or, "What was really special about Jim is the fact that he made a million dollars and I am glad the bastard is dead – because now I inherit most of it!"

And yet in our day-to-day lives is it not material goods that we define our success by? We spend our whole lives chasing material goods and yet envisioning my eulogy lets me know that these are not the most important things in hindsight.

Why then are we driven by materialism – to consume, to purchase, to own things – in our day-to-day lives?

To answer that, I ask: "Who are our teachers?"

Who are our Teachers?

Television is the greatest teacher of our time. The plug-in drug consumes our lives and energy. Here are some shocking facts:

- The TV in a typical North American household is on for about 7 hours a day[3] and the average North American spends 28 hours a week watching it.[4]
- That means Americans spend *20 million* years of human experience watching TV![5] every year.
- Kids spend more time watching TV than in school: between the ages of 6 and 18 the average child will spend 15,000 to 16,000 hours watching TV vs. 13,000 in school.[6]
- By the age of six, an average American child will already have spent more time watching TV than he/she will spend talking to his/her father in *their entire life!*
- By the time they are 20-years-old, kids have spent more time watching TV commercials than they have with their fathers!

And what are we being taught?

- By the time they leave elementary school, kids will have seen 20,000 murders and over 80,000 other assaults on TV. That's 100,000 violent acts before they're teenagers.

- The average child sees more than 20,000 TV commercials a year.

And it is not just violence that is the issue – it's consumerism. On an average day each one of us sees up to 4,000 ads – each ad telling us to consume, to consume, to consume. So we begin to define our lives in terms of material consumption. Because we see this every day, we hear this every day – we begin to think this every day. Deep within ourselves we come to feel successful only when we have the material things – the car, the BMW, the gold Cross pen.

But when we are at the end of our lives, when we're ghosts at our own funeral, all the material things vanish. And what is left? The essence of our life. And it has nothing to do with materialism. The essence of our life has to do with feelings, with emotions and with principles. Those things you can never buy. You can't buy love. You can't buy honesty. You can't buy compassion. You can't buy tolerance. You can't buy faith. You can never buy any of these things in any store. All of these are qualities or values you have to earn through the practice of emotional intelligence and the learning paradox.

What ultimately is most important to us – the values we would like to be remembered for, we can develop every day.

I have found it is very hard to change myself – to become more of who I feel I am meant to be. Where will the power come to help me transform myself? It will only come from

knowing who we want to be and then having the courage to become more of who we are meant to be.

Mental Cyanide

Would you eat out of a garbage can? Of course not! Then why would you fill your mind with garbage?[7]

I am a journalist and I had to stop reading the newspapers, stop watching television and stop listening to the radio. Why? Because they are so negative. I find it too depressing. Every day in the newspapers I can read about a mass murderer who killed 13 kids when he went mad with a handgun or an Uzi. I can read about wars, disasters and bankruptcies. In fact journalists, who have brilliant, inquisitive minds, set out to find the sickest, most twisted stories to feed us on a daily basis.

Studies have shown that if you take a "news" story and write it three different ways (journalists call these slants) the journalists will pick the most negative story – the one that highlights the most conflict, as being the best.

News is essentially negative – and it gives a biased view of reality. I have thought about it long and hard, searched my memory – and I have never known anyone who was a mass murderer – in other words I have no experience in my life relating to a mass murderer. And yet I can read about one on a daily basis. Similarly, I have never had my house flooded by rains but I can watch a flood somewhere in the world on a daily basis on TV.

This negative news gives me a skewed view of reality. What the news doesn't tell me is that six billion people woke up this morning, went to work, to school, played, ate and made love to their partners at night. It was a normal day.

Being fed a continuous diet of sensationalized destruction, murder and war is depressing and unhealthy. Stories that touch my heart – stories about love, compassion and the noble nature of humanity are considered "soft" by editors. So news is a biased view of reality.

The size of the problem has overwhelmed me in past – and I feel helpless and demoralized. I believe it is irresponsible for the media to focus so much attention on the problems and so little on the solutions.

The TV culture breeds isolation and hopelessness.

People often ask me – well if you don't read newspapers, listen to the radio or watch TV, how do you keep up with the news? Well if something is big enough – people will tell me.

Why We Pay Attention to Negative News

If you put out rat poison and a rat eats it, but doesn't eat enough to kill it, that rat will *never* eat that poison again because it will remember the smell, the taste of the poison and never go near it again. Our minds work in the same way. We remember events that have high levels of emotion tied to them with vividness. In the case of negative events, it's an evolutionary defense mechanism. That is why we remember negative things.

Addictive Society

We live in an addictive society. By definition an addiction is something that keeps us unaware of the power it has over us. TV addiction is widespread, highlighted by the frightening figures on TV viewing. Many people are addicted to news – unaware of how it alters their worldview. Consumerism is an addiction – and it is our material intensive lifestyle that is the root cause of environmental destruction. Addictions to drugs, alcohol and cigarettes are rampant as is workaholism. The addictions are too numerous to list. The only solution to a deep cultural pathology is deep cultural therapy. And this deep cultural therapy will come in the form of renewed spiritual consciousness on the personal and societal level.

Negative Emotions

If you are a heavy smoker and have to chose between giving up smoking and holding onto resentment, anger, fear and other negative emotions, from a health perspective you'll be far better off continuing to smoke! This is a surprising insight from *Emotional Intelligence.*

The word resentment comes from the Latin word resigno and French resentire – meaning to re-live or re-feel. When I resent something – a hurt done to me by someone in the past – I will often relive the hurt over and over and over again. Like an endless video loop that I play over and over again in my mind, till I whip myself up into a frenzy of self-righteous, justified, indignant anger. I don't know about you, but there are few things that I enjoy more than self-righteous, justified, indignant anger.

In *How to Succeed with People,* Stephen Covey suggests a hypothetical situation: imagine a poisonous snake bit me in the dessert. There would be two things I could do. One would be to chase after that snake with an ax and chop it up – and it would feel good because I would punish that sucker and be victorious. But in the process of chasing the snake, I would pump the venom through my system and drive it to the heart. And shortly after killing the snake, I myself would keel over and die. It would be a rather brief victory. The other thing I could do would be to let the snake go, suck out the venom, spit it on the ground and live.

At this point some people add, "and then chase the snake and kill it!" But they're missing the point.

A resentment is like the snake's venom – it poisons my relationship with people around me. Someone could have done me a wrong 10 years ago and they could actually have died in the interim, but I may still nurture that resentment.

And who is in control? It's like I have given my self-will and power over to the person I resent and say, "You are my master. I am a puppet and you are pulling my strings. You are living in my head rent-free all day!"

So when the Bible says we must forgive our enemies – it is not for *their* sake, it's for *ours!*

To Forgive is not to Forget

If someone did me some wrong, forgiving is not forgetting. Forgetting is to remain in denial and denial would enable me to continue being involved in that relationship without saying something, challenging unacceptable behavior and perhaps ending the relationship. Forgiving involves removing the entire emotional sting from the event, and then basing my reaction on my values.

Emotional Health

Negative emotions have a negative effect on our health. In *Reversing Heart Disease*, Dr. Dean Ornish outlines how he has worked with patients threatened with heart attacks requiring double, triple and quadruple bypasses but being unable to schedule their surgery quickly. Desperate and willing to try anything, these patients were willing to try Ornish's program, which involved moving to a vegan diet (eliminating all animal fats – meats, eggs, cheese and dairy products), prayer and meditation, discussion groups with peers in the same situation and exercise – beginning with walking and gradually building to more strenuous exercise over time. Ornish documented reversing heart disease. In other words, by eliminating the causes of disease (high fat and cholesterol diets, stress, struggling with emotions in isolation and lack of exercise) patients dissolved the excess cholesterol that was blocking their arteries!

Chapter 1

Proper Perspective

Imagine an actor in a play – who mistakenly thinks that he is the director of the play. He arranges all the other actors according to his view of how the play should unfold, and no sooner does he get back to his place, than some other actor has the arrogance to assume that he's the director of the play. And this second actor rearranges everyone. So the first actor redoubles his effort, again running around the stage rearranging the actors. No sooner has the first actor returned again to his place; than someone else gets the mistaken idea that they are the director.

It doesn't matter how hard the actor works; how well intentioned he is; how deeply he cares about the other players; or how positive his mental attitude. It doesn't matter how many different approaches he takes – being alternatively pleasant, angry, commanding or sullen. The actor is in for a life of frustration. His central problem – the root cause of his woes – is a faulty perception: he thinks he's the director of the play when he's only an actor.[8]

This is a powerful metaphor for life. I get angry when things don't go my way. I feel my partner should do certain things, have a certain level of tolerance for my shortcomings and she doesn't. I feel certain people should respect me and they don't. As a child I felt I should get certain presents and I didn't. In short, I am self-centered – I feel that the world should revolve around me. If people only did as I thought they should, the world would be a better place. The problem is that I assume that I am the director of the play! There is a director at work – only I don't know what the plot is, and that frustrates me.

For me, the story of the director of the play is a metaphor about self-centeredness.

As noted before, the Buddhists say that the root of all suffering is attachment. I tend to get upset when I think I am the director of the play – in other words, the world should unfold according to Jim Harris. I am "attached" to my expectations of the outcomes. An expectation is a premeditated resentment. I get upset when I am "attached" to an outcome which doesn't occur.

Whenever I am Upset, There's Something Wrong with Me

There is a simple and powerful spiritual truth: "Whenever I am upset, there is something wrong with me!"

Here's an example: I have commissioned sales agents in the US who sell my services. One time one of them made a pass at me. Now there were four things wrong with the situation as I saw it. In order of ascending importance from least to most important:

1. It's dangerous to get involved with people you work with. If the personal relationship goes sour, how will it affect the business relationship?

2. Secondly, that person was married

3. Third, I was married
4. And fourth, he was a guy. "Not that there's anything wrong with that!" as Jerry Seinfeld would say.

Now of all the problems it was the fourth that was bothering me the most. Then he began to call me at home – and say, "You're in Philadelphia next week giving a presentation, what color of markers would you like?" Clearly he just wanted to talk. I was getting more upset.

Back to the principle, "Whenever I am upset, there is something wrong with me." What could be wrong with me? I mean, he made the pass at me. He's calling me at home. He is harassing me.

I had to really think about it. Reflect and meditate on it. What was my part in all this? Well I hadn't told him that I was uncomfortable or asked him to stop calling me. Why not? Well first off we Canadians want everyone to like us – so we tend to not like confrontation. Secondly at that point US business represented about 40 percent of my revenue. If I confronted him and it didn't go well, I might lose that agent and the revenue. So my part was fear and fear of financial insecurity – or the flip side is lack of courage and lack of faith – faith that if the confrontation didn't go well, I wouldn't find a better agent. So I prayed about it, developed the courage, confronted him over the phone and he denied everything. The calls stopped and we get along very well today.

I can't control everything that happens, but I can control how I react to situations. The principle of "whenever I am upset, there is something wrong with me" means that I have to take responsibility whenever I am upset and look at why I am upset and how my own thinking and my own actions are contributing to it. It's far easier to be a victim and to blame them – whoever they are – for what they are doing to me. It's a powerful insight – *perhaps the largest challenges I face in life are my own fears!*

How do I develop stronger courage? Only by facing situations I fear! How can I develop greater patience? Only by living calmly through situations where I am impatient. So I must be careful what I ask for!

The Value of Pain

Very few people think of it this way, but pain can be very useful. In *When Bad Things Happen to Good People* Harold Kushner writes:

Approximately one out of every 400,000 babies born is fated to live a short, pitiful life which none of us would envy, a life in which he will frequently hurt himself, sometimes seriously, and not know it. That child has a rare genetic disease known as *familial dysautonomia*. He cannot feel pain. Such a child will cut himself, burn himself, fall down and break a bone, and never know that something is wrong. He will not complain of sore throats and aches, and his parents will not know he is sick until it is too late.[9]

Pain is one of the gifts of life. I am not talking about the pain that people feel in car accidents or with fatal cancers. I am talking about the pain we often feel in life, such as when we are fired from a job, or lose a relationship. Perhaps there is a lesson I have to learn, such as being sensitive to other people. Or perhaps I have to learn that I am more than my job, more than my relationships.

In a strange way, pain is a friend and a teacher. It is what stimulates us or motivates us to learn and grow. It forces us to move on. It pushes us out of our comfort zone. In fact, I might never move were it not for pain. Pain is built into the game of life. It is not that there is a right or a wrong, just that when we are in pain something is wrong.

The real question is can we make sense or purpose out of pain? Kushner writes:

> The pain of giving birth is creative pain. It is pain that has meaning, pain that gives life that leads to something. That is why the person who gives birth is willing to do it again. That is why the person who passes a kidney stone will usually say "I'd give anything not to have to go through that again," but the woman who has given birth to a child, like the runner or mountain climber who has driven their body to reach a goal, can transcend their pain and contemplate repeating the experience.[10]

Little Death: Big Death

Many people are afraid of the pain of confrontation. They fear confronting others for fear of hurting their feelings or hurting the relationship. And so we save up these resentments towards other people until we blow up and fire the employee, quit the job, or say something we later regret. I call this little death, big death. Because we fear the confrontation (little death) we store up our resentments and anger until we end the relationship (big death). But in fact, because we have never been honest about our feelings, we haven't given the other person a fair opportunity to change. We've expected them to be a mind reader. And then feel justified for firing them, quitting or ending the relationship.

Separate Action from Outcome

I need to separate *action* from *outcome*, or to put it another way, I have to separate the *process* or *discipline* from the *outcome*. By following the process the outcome will follow. Or think about it as being able to create luck!

Creating Luck

Some people tell me, "You're really lucky." In some sense it's true – I've been blessed in my life, but in another sense, I believe we can create our own luck, when we understand the deeper underlying structures of success.

After university I traveled around the world for four years. I returned to Canada in 1988 and I swore I would have a job, any job, within a week. So I got one as a telemarketer. I hated it. I was selling subscriptions to the *Financial Post* (FP) – Canada's national financial newspaper. As telemarketers, we called people on lists provided by the firm, but those answering the phone typically didn't own stocks, or subscribe to a daily newspaper let alone a financial one. It was hard, frustrating work, and if you sold three subscriptions a day you were doing very well.

So I began to ask, "Who would *want* to buy the *Financial Post*?" The obvious answer was stockbrokers. They work in the markets. They knew the FP, so I wouldn't have to explain what it was, or convince them of the value of the promotional offer. Through research I discovered that every brokerage firm has to publish the list of all its directors. I obtained the list from the stock exchange and began calling directors.

My sales exploded. On a single call I sold seven subscriptions because I got a floor trader who yelled out the offer to everyone else on the trading desk. I set new records for the highest ever daily, weekly and monthly sales for the telemarketing firm. The achievement had nothing to do with my selling skills and everything to do with thinking about how to increase the odds of sales success.

Funnel Theory

I never intended to remain a telemarketer – so during days off, evenings and weekends I applied for over 300 jobs. Some were in response to advertised positions; others were unsolicited and aimed at companies I thought I would enjoy working for. From the 300 applications, I was invited to 12 interviews and offered six positions, four of which I found interesting. And of these I picked the one that I found most exciting – working as a researcher on *The 100 Best Companies to Work for in Canada* at the *Financial Post.*

After working on the book for a year, I was made a co-author. So by the time I was 30 I had a national bestseller to my name. Co-authoring the book changed my life because it led me to becoming a professional speaker at conferences and seminars.

In this case, understanding the underlying structure of success means appreciating the ratios: 300:12:6:4:1. If I had only applied to 100 jobs I would have only had four interviews, two offers and one of interest, so I would have had no choice. Had I only applied to 50 positions, I may have only been invited to two interviews and not received any offers. It's a numbers game.

A second lesson is *it's not personal.* Many people take rejection personally. In my case I received 288 rejections out of 300 applications. Because I understood the dynamic of the system, I didn't take it personally. During the early 1990's a typical newspaper ad for a job opening generated over 100 applications, so my chance of success to begin with was one in a hundred. Taking a rejection personally when the odds of success were only one percent would have been setting myself up for failure.

Ninety percent of the success in life is just showing up.

Woody Allen

Systems and structures determine outcomes. This was the essence of W. Edwards Deming's teachings and that of systems dynamic thinkers, such as Peter Senge, author of *The Fifth Discipline*. I need to think beyond my own involvement and understand the system dynamics in play. This thinking is fundamental to achieving success in any business.

Organizing Successful Events

The same law applies to organizing events. The success or failure of a political rally has nothing to do with the number of people who turn out and everything to do with the size of the room. If 150 people turn out to a political rally in a hall that holds 1,000, the media will report that the event was a failure. However, if 150 people turn out and the room only holds 100, the media will report – "In a standing room only crowd, the campaign launch was a tremendous success. In fact, people were standing at the door eagerly listening to the candidate, who was overwhelmed by the turn-out and taken aback by the depth of support." TV cameras will show people squeezed together shoulder to shoulder straining to hear the candidate. Success or failure has nothing to do with the turn-out and everything to do with room size. Good political candidates don't take events with a poor turn out personally because they know the organizer selected too large a room.

This philosophy applies to hosting a party. The number of people who attend a party has nothing to do with how much people like you, it has everything to do with the number of people you invite. So if you want to have 50 people at your party, you'll have to invite 150. A number of other factors will affect turn out, such as the day of the week (more people go away for weekends), the season (during holiday seasons you'll be competing with other parties), the age of your friends (those with new babies tend not to go out), the weather (in winter people are less likely to go out), whether you only tell people or give them a printed invitation (printed invites increase attendance because people have a reminder), follow up e-mails increase attendance, and the type of occasion (if people say they are coming to your party they don't feel committed, but a dinner party has a higher level of commitment and a wedding the greatest). Even if people have RSVPed, you have to account for a certain number of no shows. Airlines know this, which is why they overbook flights. The key to being a successful host or hostess is knowing the system and then planning accordingly.

The key to exceeding expectations is setting them properly in the first place. If you are hosting a party and you have invited 150 people – and someone asks how many are coming? Answer 40 people. When 50 show up they'll think you're popular. If on the other hand you tell them you have invited 150 people and only 50 show up they will feel sorry for you. Perception is everything.

Success is not necessarily due to brilliance, but changing the odds of success.

Weddings

Think of your own experience – do weddings typically come in on budget, under budget or over budget? Invariably it's over budget. By how much? Ten percent? Twenty percent? I have had people in seminars reply as much as 250 percent! In asking this question to participants around the world, I think the average is probably 30-40 percent over budget. Well if you know that a wedding is going to come in at 40 percent over budget – and you want to spend $20,000, then plan to have a $14,000 wedding – and with the cost over runs you'll have a $20,000 one.

The same is true of projects. Do change initiatives within organizations typically take more or less time than planned? Run over or under budget? By how much? Do projects usually deliver all the promised features? Or is some percentage inevitably still missing.

If experience shows that these are classic patterns, project managers, executives and entrepreneurs need to take this into account in planning for success.

Discipline = Freedom

While it seems a paradox, it is through discipline we achieve freedom. It is the discipline of understanding the underlying system, and then working with it that creates success. Do your kids always want to stay up late? Most parents answer, "Yes." Well then, why get upset when they ask? If you know in advance something is going to happen, don't get upset. Expect it.

Nine publishers rejected JK Rowling's *Harry Potter and the Philosopher's Stone* before a small UK publisher, Bloomsbury, bought it. The Harry Potter series has created a publishing phenomenon selling over 113 million copies worldwide and encouraging millions of children to read. Thirty-three publishers rejected *Chicken Soup for the Soul* before it was accepted. The rejection letters said things like, "The book is too positive," and "Anthologies don't sell." John Grisham's *A Time to Kill* was turned down 28 times, and even *Gone With the Wind* suffered 25 rejections.

Paradoxically, freedom comes from discipline. The freedom is not found in following the whim of emotion. Many people feel that being spontaneous is real freedom. Imagine being "spontaneous" when making decisions in building your dream home! Discipline gives me the ultimate freedom. The discipline of planning, the discipline of execution, the discipline of consistency in the face of setback. It is discipline that gives us the ultimate feelings of satisfaction. In this context then, I can be spontaneous. It is not an either or because living in response to emotions or whims is not freedom. It is enslaving.

True freedom requires a discipline to apply the philosophy of the Taoist Farmer. We can't control life, but we can control our reaction to life. Having the discipline to make the best out of every situation is a rare gift, but we must work to develop it.

Antonio Gramsci (1891-1937) was an intellectual, writer, member of the Italian parliament, and general secretary of the underground Italian Communist party. He was a labor organizer and Mussolini had him arrested in 1926, because the fascist leader felt his ideas were a threat to the state. Gramsci spent the last 11 years of his life in prison. While in prison he wrote 33 notebooks containing almost 3,000 pages. Known as the *Prison Notebooks*, his writings were smuggled out of prison by family and friends. Had he not been arrested we would never have known of Gramsci's work because he had been too busy organizing until he was jailed. How can something good come out of a bad situation? It all depends on how you look at the situation.

Or think about Nelson Mandela who spent twenty-seven years in prison. When he was released, he became president of South Africa. He created the Truth and Reconciliation Commission to uncover the truth about the horrors that occurred under apartheid and then to reconcile the nation. Anyone who testified before the commission was given amnesty for any past crimes they admitted to at the commission. Where do you get the power, the strength to forgive after 27 years of your life has been taken away? Very few people have the luxury of spending 27 years developing spiritually through prayer and meditation – to generate the strength that Nelson Mandela exhibited.

Discipline of Love

Love is both a verb (action) and a noun (feeling). People often confuse the two. When we talk of love, we are often talking about the feeling (noun) – a sense of joy, bliss, well-being and caring for someone else. But paradoxically, the only way to gain the feeling is through the action.

Shawnessy Johnson, our Web designer and chief marketer at Strategic Advantage, just gave birth to her first child – Spencer McKenzie Johnson Band. For Shawnessy the action of love (verb) – involves getting up in the middle of the night to feed Spencer, change his diaper, and soothe him if he is crying. She engages in the *actions* of love regardless of her sleep depravation or *feelings*. In other words, mothers show love in their action despite not always having the feeling.

In the same way, people confuse the feeling of peace (noun) with the verb of peace. Being peaceful means being loving towards others whom we often might not like.

Motivating People
Quick Wins

In *Rules for Radicals*, Saul Alinsky, an organizer who campaigned on social justice issues in the 1960s, outlines his philosophy. Judo embraces the philosophy of using your opponent's strength against them. Alinsky worked the same way.

Lets take an imaginary scenario, of getting a bank to hire African Americans. In designing a campaign, Alinsky might get 200 volunteers to line up at the bank. When each individual got to the front of the line up he or she would open an account with five dollars. Then they'd go to the back of the line. After the long wait of getting to the front of the line, they'd withdraw a dollar and then go to the back of the line up.

This process would ensure the bank's regular customers would never get to do their banking, because most people are unwilling to wait in a 200 person line up.

A bank's very purpose is to open accounts and let customers deposit and withdraw their funds – and such activities are entirely legal. If Alinsky's protest goaded the bank manager into a rash decision, such as asking the police to arrest all the protestors, imagine the headlines the next day "Bank has Police Arrest 200 for Opening Accounts."

Because the bank would feel helpless in fighting the protest it would likely quickly give into the demands and begin hiring African Americans.

Alinsky always worked within the system to create quick and early wins. The lesson here for leaders is that it's important to help people realize quickly that they can be successful. Or in other words, create quick wins.

Setting Expectations Properly

The second rule of motivation would be set expectations correctly. The key to exceeding people's expectations is setting them properly in the first place.

If your car isn't working and you take it into your mechanic and he says he'll be able to fix it for $400 and when you pick up the car you find the bill is $600 you'll be upset. However, if he says it'll be $800 and you come back and find it's only $600 you'll be delighted. You paid the same amount in both cases – but your expectations were different.

People often set unrealistic expectations when they begin a project. And when they don't see the results immediately, they quit in discouragement.

Unconditional Support & High Expectations

Dennis Waitley, author of *The Psychology of Winning*, tells of an experiment that highlights the importance of expectations. Three high school teachers were called into the principal's office and told they had been specially selected to participate in a secret experiment because they were the best teachers in the school. The classes they were going to be assigned in the fall would be made up of the brightest pupils. At the end of the year, the progress of their students would be compared with that of average students in the school. But the teachers were not allowed to tell anyone else – the students, parents or other teachers.

These teachers were excited. They spent the year fostering and nurturing their students. In everything they did, their expectations shone through, "You are the best. You are the brightest. You will excel." Sure enough, at the end of the year, the progress these students had made was phenomenal. It was better than that of the students in the rest of the school, the area and the state. The teachers, who were proud, said, "Well, it's a fantastic achievement, but then our students are the best in the school."

The teachers were staggered when they found out that their students had only been average, randomly selected from the student body.

But after reflecting for a minute the three teachers perked up, "Well, that's understandable. We're the best teachers!"

"No," came the reply, "your names were randomly selected from a hat containing the names of all teachers in the school."

The teachers *believed* their students were the best, and so they *became* the best. Belief, or expectation, is a powerful force. Creating high expectations – believing in people and their inherent capacity to do well – is a powerful motivator.

If you really believe you are the best, you are forced to live up to that image.

Don't just aim to live a full and exciting life. Expect that it will be, and make all decisions based on what you would do if you were living the most exciting, fulfilling life.

Allow Enough Time

When you plant Chinese Bamboo nothing happens in the first year. You water it, fertilize it and still nothing happens. In the second year, nothing happens, even though you've carefully watered and fertilized it. You begin to worry, "Does it have enough sunshine? Has there been enough rain?" In the third year, nothing happens. The fourth year it's the same! You wonder, "Did I buy a genetically deficient bamboo?"

Then in the fifth year, in the course of just six weeks, the bamboo grows 90 feet! Bamboo is one of the fastest growing plants in the world and can grow up to three feet in a 24-hour period.

The question is, did the Chinese Bamboo take six weeks or five years to grow 90 feet?

The answer is five years. In the first four years all the energy was spent laying the root system that would support the stunning growth. The same is true of many things in life.

In the rush for success are we building foundations on sand? Or are we taking time to ensure the organization we are building is for the long term? In some cases fast is slow and slow is fast.

The Chinese Bamboo story lets me know that things are often hard in the beginning. For instance, a NASA rocket spends more energy in the first few minutes of take off, breaking the bonds of the earth's gravitational force, than in the rest of its journey, traveling millions of miles through space and returning to earth.

The Chinese Bamboo tells me that actions are often separated from results for a significant period of time. The time, love and energy that parents invest in their children may not become apparent for years. This has generated a powerful insight for me: most of us will never know in our lifetime what our true legacy is.

Working with Others

A saying that I find powerful is, "We meet together as saints and yet we are all separate as sinners." meaning that we always share with each other our successes, but we remain isolated with our failures.

The Polynesian Indians have a ceremony that they conduct by standing on opposite sides of a fire. They say, "I give you my red, you give me your yellow," meaning – I share with you my weakness and you share with me your strength. This seems to be the opposite of how we typically work with each other – we only share our successes. In being honest with others and sharing with them the difficulties I initially had in starting my business, I may be able to help set their expectations properly.

If I am trying to help a new person start their business are they going to get it as fast as I would expect or like? Likely not. I can't keep ripping up the plant to see how the roots are doing. So in some sense leadership is all about having patience to let people develop at their own speed.

Summary

On the road to success setbacks and rejection are guaranteed. True success involves understanding this in advance, being persistent in the face of adversity, and changing the odds through our actions to "create" our own luck.

Chapter Two

The Learning Paradox

The Learning Paradox

Eighty percent of the technology we will use in our day-to-day lives in the next 10 years has yet to be invented! If you find this hard to believe, think about how quickly technology is changing. The Web was created by the release of *Mosaic* in 1993 and now eCommerce is estimated to grow to $6.78 trillion by 2004![12] So in less than one decade the Web will have had the most profound technological impact on human society in history. Amazon.com, founded in June 1995, had more than $3.12 billion of sales in 2001, becoming the third largest bookstore in the world by sales! Here are some predictions:

- Long distance rates will fall to three cents a minute by 2005 and will be free by 2007. How do you get free long distance? It will be the lost leader that a telco gives you when you sign up for a multi year bundled service – getting your local calls, calling features, long distance, cell phone, Internet connection, video-on-demand, and pager all from one company.
- E-commerce will have saved organizations over $1.25 trillion by 2003!

- Microsoft assumes that the average size of a hard drive today will be the amount of RAM on an "average" PC in seven years. In 2002, the average hard drive on a new PC was 60 gigabytes – imagine having 60 gigs of RAM on an "average" PC in 2009 – a really hot system might have 80 or 100 gigs of RAM!
- In 10 years time, a standard PC will be 100 times more powerful than an average PC today.
- We will have free, full screen, full motion video conferencing on desktops by 2005 across the Web. It will be the same quality as watching TV (30 frames a second); in 2002 the technology was still jerky and in small frame.

The rapid increase in computing power and the explosion of the Web will profoundly affect the way all organizations work. People often ask, "Why would we need such powerful computers? What would we use them for?" Applications will be fundamentally different:

- Voice recognition will be integrated into most computer applications. I use *Dragon NaturallySpeaking* – a software program that allows my computer to take dictation at 160 words per minute with 99 percent accuracy! I simply wear a microphone headset and chat away. I predict that the Graphical User Interface (GUI) will give way to AUI – the Audio User Interface – and like Jean Luc Picard of *Star Trek*, by 2010 we will predominantly interact with computers by talking to them.

- By 2010 we will have real time, instantaneous simultaneous, international translation – so you will be able to speak to your computer in English, and someone in Japan will watch your mouth moving but will hear Japanese. Similarly when you hear them speak it will be in English.

With so much change, how can individuals create job security? How can organizations keep their market share?

Job security today is based on learning, changing and accepting uncertainty. Paradoxically, these are what we, as adults fear the most! We have moved from a knowledge-based to a learning-based economy. This is the theme of *The Learning Paradox.*

Gaining Comfort from Discomfort

When I address conferences and seminars, I ask participants to write down their names as fast as they can three times. Then I ask them to switch hands and repeat the exercise.

At this point there is usually a lot of laughter. When I ask how it feels to write with the "other" hand, I get comments like, "Awkward!" "Frustrating!" "Clumsy!" One man said, "When I was writing the first time, I felt like a lawyer; the second time like a doctor."

Next I ask, "How would you feel if I told you that you

had to write with your other hand for the entire day back at the office?" Typical answers are, "I'd take the day off!" "Stressed!" "Anxious!"

Then I ask, "How about if you had to write with the other hand for the next week?" Responses include, "I'd take holidays!" "Do you expect me to keep serving the same number of customers?" "I'd dictate!" "I'd delegate!" "I'd start typing!" "My productivity would plummet."

Finally I ask, "What if I told you, that you had to write with the other hand for the rest of your life?" People typically are resistant: "I can hardly wait to retire!" "What's in it for me?" "Why?" "Who are you to say?"

Some are accepting: "Well, I guess I'd learn."

Most of us are addicted to feeling competent. We are uncomfortable when we feel incompetent. We like the feeling of knowing.

If you can become comfortable with the discomfort you feel when learning new skills – if you can become accustomed to the discomfort that change brings, then you will never have to worry about job security for the rest of your life!

Job Security in Past

What created security in the past? If you wanted job security what kind of company did you want to work for? What were the characteristics of a secure position? Just for fun, I ask audiences to put their answers in words beginning with the letter "S". Typically, people suggest the following categories:

Size of Organization Security was a function of the size of the organization you worked for. If you landed a job with IBM or the government and worked hard, you never had to worry about the future.

Share of Market If you worked for a corporate leader with dominant market share, such as Coca-Cola, Procter & Gamble or monopolies such as utility companies, you were more secure.

Stability of Industry/Company If you had a job in a stable company in a stable industry such as insurance or banking, you had a job for life.

Salary and Benefits Many people worked for companies that offered good pay and benefits. If you were loyal, worked hard and didn't question authority, you could depend on regular salary increases. Upon retirement you could count on the company pension plan.

Status of Position The higher up you were in the corporate hierarchy, the more secure you were.

Service The longer you worked for a company, the more secure you were. After 40 years you could expect to retire with a gold watch awarded to you at the president's annual dinner.

Seniority Unions created security. Once you got into a closed shop, you were home free. The stronger the union, the more secure your job.

Specialized Knowledge If you had a PhD, MBA or

specialized knowledge, you were more secure.

Specialized Function If you had a specialized function – mainframe guru, for example – you were more secure because the organization depended on you.

Over the years, I have had some funny answers:

Sex "What do you mean? Gender – i.e. men got ahead of women faster? The glass ceiling – the invisible barrier that prevents equality in the most senior ranks of Fortune 500 companies? Sometimes this was what the participant meant, other times it wasn't.

Son or Daughter of the owner.

Suck Up As long as you told the boss what he wanted to hear, you were secure.

New Rules

I argue that everything that used to create job security in the past now creates insecurity:

Size IBM once prided itself on offering employees lifetime security. But between 1989 and 1995, IBM laid off 200,000 people – half of its worldwide workforce. In fact, large companies have been the largest net job losers! Large corporations were once considered immune to market forces. Clearly, they aren't offering the security they used to.

Share In 1997, *Fortune* magazine proclaimed that Coca-Cola was America's most admired company and that "brands rule."[13] However, not even Coke has been immune to crushing market shifts. Coca-Cola has been hurt badly by private-label soda bottlers, most noticeably Cott. Wal-Mart annually sells over a billion cans of *Sam's Choice* soda produced by Cott. In Canada, Cott has cornered 26 percent of all supermarket soda sales.[14] Coke's profit has been so eroded that the company closed its Canadian head office in 1995 and now runs the Canadian operations out of Atlanta. Market share is less secure than ever. Competition is coming from unexpected sources and from small, cost-effective and highly focused companies.

Stability The less your industry is changing; the more it is at risk of being blindsided. A study by Royal Dutch/Shell found that between 1979 and 1994, 40 percent of *Fortune 500* companies ceased to exist. Some were acquired or merged, while others simply failed to keep up with the changing times and lost their leadership positions. If you work for a bank and they're still doing banking the way they did it in 1990, I argue your organization is due for one big shake up. Stability is a predictor of insecurity, not security.

Salary and Benefits It used to be that if you worked for the government you just had to show up every day, have a pulse and you would automatically get a cost of living allowance increase every year. At one seminar a man yelled out, "a pulse was optional." But today we don't get increases just for showing up. Today it is performance that counts. Compensation is based on performance.

Status The higher you go, the thinner the air gets! The

more senior you are, the more performance counts.

Service If you have been in the same position for 30 years and have learned no new skills, I argue you are more likely to get a pink slip than a gold watch. Research shows that on average, today's workers will hold 10 different positions in three different fields over their work life.

Seniority Who has the skills that will help the organization transform itself for the future? The 18-year-old who surfs the Web every night, or the 55-year-old union member who doesn't know how to turn on the computer? Based on seniority (last in, first out) in a downsizing situation, who will the union push out of the organization? The 18-year-old. In other words, the union will push out the very employees who possess the new skills necessary to help create a viable organization for the future.

Old-style unions typically oppose cross-functional job sharing and training. Which member is more secure – one who has only worked in a narrow job description for 25 years or one who has worked in four different positions over eight years?

Specialized Knowledge We are more educated than ever before. North American business schools turn out over 100,000 MBAs a year, and 250,000 business degree grads.[15] But in times of rapid change, knowledge depreciates in value just as quickly as computers and software technologies. Knowledge counts, but the right attitude and a commitment to lifelong learning is more important. A PhD could simply mean you know a lot about old stuff. Stephen Covey points out:[16]

> Education's main value does not lie in getting knowledge, much of which will be obsolete sooner or later. It certainly doesn't lie in credits earned or degrees conferred. These may open doors of opportunity but only real competence will keep them open. In fact, in our rapidly changing world there is no "future," no economic security in any job or situation. The only real economic security lies within the person, in his competence and power to produce.
>
> Education's main value lies in learning how to continually learn, how to think and to communicate, how to appreciate and to produce, how to adapt to changing realities without sacrificing changeless values. Result? An inner confidence in the basic ability to cope successfully with whatever life brings.

Specialized Function Assembly-line workers, bank tellers, typesetters, telephone operators, receptionists and even mainframe programmers – every time you turn around, another job function is being threatened. If your job is being replaced by technology or restructuring, how can you feel secure? Specialized knowledge, while still important, no longer provides the long-term security it once did.

Social Contract The old social contract of working hard and never questioning authority in return for security is dangerous. Workaholism was encouraged. Today people want more "balanced" lives. In the future, I predict it will be a status symbol to hold a significant position of leadership, perform exceptionally and work only 40 hours a week!

Finally, never questioning those in positions of authority creates insecurity. To thrive today, organizations must promote open, honest and vigorous internal debate. Employees should be encouraged to challenge decisions they believe are wrong. None of us knows what the future holds. Creating new value for customers requires a corporate culture in which open, honest debate can occur and where employees can challenge management decisions without fear of recrimination. Serving the hierarchy must be subordinated to serving the customer. One executive coined the phrase, "the egoless corporation" to emphasize how today no individual has a monopoly on insight. Organizations need to draw upon the full intellectual talents of all employees. The sign of an excellent place to work is one in which there is healthy, vigorous and open debate.

Speed Complacency kills. Even in rapidly expanding industries there is little job security. Let's look at the fastest-growing industry sector worldwide: computer software. This sector has grown by 30 percent in real terms, compounded annually between 1980 and 1995. Yet, even in this explosive industry there is no security. *Information Week* annually ranks the 500 most innovative corporate users of information technology. More than half the computer companies on the 1995 list did not appear on the

2000 list! Some were sold, others fell behind and a few went belly-up. In short, even the vaunted computer market is uncertain.[17]

If everything that used to create job security now creates insecurity – what will create security for people in this new, rapidly changing environment?

Learning as Play; Life as Challenge

I like to think of life as a video game. I think it's an apt metaphor for the business environment we find ourselves in.

Many children today play video games. Parents describe their kids as "intense," "challenged," "excited" and "obsessed" when they receive a new game. A mother once commented that her son was "deaf" while a father said, "unable to mow the lawn!"

Do kids read the manual before they begin? As one mother put it, "I'm the one who reads the manual." Children show no fear while learning.

Have you seen or heard of any courses such as *Game Boy for Advanced Users?* Or *Xbox 101?* Or have you seen that bestseller *PlayStation for Dummies?* Of course not. After one presentation, a woman came up to me and said, "You mentioned those Dummies books in your talk – I just want to let you know that they are WAY TOO FAR ADVANCED! What I want is a computer book for real, bloody idiots!" So how do kids learn? By doing. By trial and error. How many times are kids willing to make mistakes?

As many times as it takes to learn.

To play a video game, a child must develop certain competencies at Level One. Once mastered, the child moves on to Level Two, where new challenges require the development of new skills. As soon as these are acquired, the child progresses to Level Three, which presents more complex challenges requiring even higher levels of skill. To keep a child's attention, game designers make each level more difficult. One tactic is to require players to develop skills that are the opposite of those needed at a lower level. That is, the very moves that allowed them to escape the challenges of Level One cause their character to die at Level Three. Unless they can *unlearn* what made them successful at Level One and learn new skills, they will not progress. As much as we need to learn, we also have to unlearn.

How else do kids learn? Their peers. I once had a father come up to me in a break and tell me, "My son went into his grade four class last week and said, 'A dozen doughnuts for anyone who can show me how to get to Level Six of the game from Level Five!'"

Each time a new challenge is overcome, a new problem presents itself. At every stage the child is challenged to learn new skills. At seminars, I ask the audience, "What happens once the child has mastered all six levels?" They answer, "They show all their friends." "They stop playing." "They chuck the game." "They trade it or sell it."

This reveals a simple but powerful insight: *Challenge is*

one of the greatest human motivators. This is the second aspect of the learning paradox: (the first aspect is that our future security is based on what we fear most – learning, changing and accepting uncertainty.) Facing our fear provides our deepest sense of satisfaction.

I challenge you to think of some time in your life when you were the proudest. Upon reflection, I am sure that you will find it was when you undertook some challenge you didn't know how to overcome. But through hard work, trial and error, perseverance and networking with colleagues, you whipped it. You got the "YES!" high-five feeling that kids get when they master all levels of the video game.

Learning a video game is a powerful metaphor for change in business. Whether new or established, organizations require progressively different competencies. At every stage of growth, new problems are encountered that will limit development unless they are overcome.

With a new business, capital is often the first limiting factor. So the entrepreneur works out of his basement, puts in sweat equity, buys second-hand furniture and equipment and generally keeps costs to the bone. So what's the next challenge? Time. Yes the entrepreneur is doing everything – accounts receivable, payable, product development, customer service, shipping, logistics, and post office mail runs. So as cash flow increases, the entrepreneur hires some people. But because cash flow is tight, he hires very inexperienced people because the wages are low. That gives rise to the need for training. So the entrepreneur invests in training, to the point where employees are now worth $17 an hour but because the entrepreneur is cheap he is paying only $13 an hour. What happens? They leave – you know, the only thing worse than training people and having them leave is not training them and having them stay! So the entrepreneur learns he must not only invest in people, but also pay fair market wages. After that, it may be necessary to focus on marketing. From the founder's basement, the company may be forced to lease office space, hire more staff, introduce benefit programs, acquire more equipment and so on and so on. Every level of development presents a new set of challenges.

Imagine, for example, that a manufacturer launches a new product with an aggressive advertising campaign in an effort to increase market share. The campaign is so successful that demand exceeds the company's production capacity. This results in long delivery delays for customers. The company must increase production capacity, maintain sufficient inventory levels and more accurately forecast market demand.

As soon as one limiting factor is addressed, a new one will arise. Suppose the company responds to increasing demand by hastily building new production facilities and rushing products to market. What suffers? Quality. So now the answer is an ISO 9000 certification. A half million dollars later the organization is certified but has introduced all sorts of paperwork. What's the new problem? Winning back customers who defected because of delays and poor quality products. The company may respond by lowering prices in an attempt to win back disgruntled customers.

But now there is a new problem. When the new production line was built, the company required additional volume to cover costs. Rather than have the line sit idle, sales reps were given incentives to increase volume, even with low-margin business, thereby amortizing the cost of the new line. This strategy lowered the per-unit cost of production. Compensation systems were designed to reward sales reps based on volume. The results were so successful that after a few years the company experienced another capacity crunch. Peak volumes were again losing the company business.

The solution to one problem has now become a new problem. Now that the line is at full capacity, the company needs a new strategy: drop the high-volume, low-margin business and concentrate on the lower-volume, high-margins and niche markets.

As the business booms and profit margins rise, the sector becomes more attractive to competitors. Competition may become the primary problem. As soon as this problem is addressed, another one will crop up, guaranteed.

Once any limiting factor is overcome, a new limiting factor will arise. Put another way, solving any problem will, over time, create a new problem in any business. The problems will not necessarily be linked, but they will always emerge. There will always be problems and challenges in business.

As in the video game, businesses graduate to higher and higher levels and the problems become more and more complex. The problems challenge us to think in new ways – ways that were not previously required and that may in fact be the opposite of those that worked at lower levels. The interaction of the various forces may also be less apparent.

So why is this important? Because people have a deep yearning for the answer. They think – if I could just get this marketing problem solved and win more market share, THEN all my problems would go away. And no sooner is the marketing problem solved than now we have to focus on production? I thought marketing would solve all our problems. Inevitably people are refocused on the new challenge – "Okay, if we can just get production under control – then everything will be great." You see we are unaware that our real problem is our mindset of thinking that one strategy, system, product or service will solve all our problems. Instead we need to focus on building our tolerance for ambiguity and complexity – becoming more flexible, creative and willing to continually change.

The Entrepreneur

At the very start of a business, the entrepreneur is involved in every decision. That's what created success

(Level One). But now that the company has grown to 100 people (Level 17), the entrepreneur's involvement in every decision is the problem. Have you ever noticed that bottlenecks are always at the top of the bottle? In other words, what made the company thrive at Level One could cause the company to fail at Level Three. So as much as we need to create learning organizations, we also need to foster unlearning organizations. To progress and develop, we must also be prepared to unlearn or let go of practices that may have been key to our past success!

To grow and change, an entrepreneur must accept that his or her greatest strengths from yesterday could become his or her greatest weaknesses today. When a snake sheds its skin, it gives up its tough, old armor for a soft but flexible covering. The old skin wasn't working but the new skin isn't working either. The snake must live through the vulnerable time – similar to writing with the other hand. Even in our personal lives, we must be prepared to evaluate old attitudes and replace them, if necessary, with ones that work better in the present. This will ultimately make our lives happier and more fulfilling.

The business "video game" ends only if the company ends. As a company continues to grow, the systems and structures become more elaborate, more complex and more cumbersome. Sometimes, these systems prevent the organization from being able to respond effectively to change – bureaucracy chokes the lifeblood out of the organization. The company has come full circle. It needs to be more entrepreneurial, not in the old style when the entrepreneur did the accounting on the back of envelopes, but in a way that focuses on the customer and strategic growth, and allows for flexibility with enough checks and balances to avoid fatal mistakes.

Daughter Learning to Walk

This notion of life being a game is equally valid when applied to our private lives. I don't have any kids, but I do have an active imagination – and I imagine that I have a nine-month-old daughter who is just learning to walk. She takes her first tentative step, wobbles and falls over. What would you do as a parent? You'd probably pick her up, give her a big hug, encourage her to try again and praise her. "Honey, grab the video camera! She walked! Call Granny!"

What would you not do as a parent? Stand over her, lean down and yell, "I have seen many first steps in my time. That was *THE WORST FIRST STEP EVER!*" No parent would ridicule her for trying. Her setbacks would be treated with love and encouragement and enthusiasm.

No matter what our age, when we are learning and growing we will stumble and fall periodically. If we are always beating ourselves up or being beaten up by others for making mistakes, we will learn more slowly. Children who are punished every time they fall will grow up to be insecure. If we are perfectionists by nature, we often set unattainable goals and beat ourselves up when we fail to reach them. Even when we come close, we are not happy. Inwardly, we will always be punishing ourselves for making mistakes even though it is impossible to learn anything new without failures.

Now imagine that time has passed and this daughter is now two years old. Whenever I come home she runs up to me and throws her arms around my legs and calls me "Daddy" and it makes my heart melt. I call her "My little Princess," and she thinks I am wonderful. But two-year-olds are a real challenge. It has been difficult for me, I've had to learn to be firm – you can't negotiate with a two-year-old or she'll run your life. And it's very trying at times having a two-year-old. I have had to learn tolerance and patience, and persistence. So I've worked hard to develop this fantastic relationship. However, I remain frozen in time. I don't change as a parent, and two years pass. She's now four but I treat her exactly as I treated her when she was two. After all, I'd perfected the relationship and it worked. How is the relationship going now – is it stronger or weaker? Someone once said, "She has you wrapped around her little finger."

She's now ten years old and I treat her exactly as I did when she was four. How are things going now? Happy or tense? She's 16 and I treat her as I did when she was 10. What's the relationship like? I get answers like, "What relationship?" "She isn't talking to you." "She has left home." "You've left home." "She's joined a biker gang." "Got a tattoo." "She's pregnant and you're about to become a grandparent."

But this is very difficult for both of us. We're both continually venturing into the future, uncertain of how to behave, uncertain of how to create a meaningful relationship. I've never had a two-year-old before. I don't know how to treat her.

For those of you who are parents, think back to your own case. You were always questioning yourself, "Is she getting to bed at the right time? Is she spending enough time with other kids? Is she watching too much TV? Are my expectations too high? Am I too permissive? What is the right balance?" You are learning at every stage of the child's development. And no sooner do you start to feel that everything is under control because you have perfected the relationship at a certain age, than she grows and new challenges arise. The relationship is characterized by periods of stability and then instability when you feel out of control again. At every stage of this growing relationship you must continually question yourself and work through the dynamics of the evolving, uncertain future. You must continually learn, change and accept uncertainty. Adolescence is a particularly difficult time. After all, we have all read those national surveys in magazines showing that kids today are having sex at 13 and 14 – but not my little Princess!

And it's equally difficult for your daughter. She is facing new situations and new peer pressure. She is starting to date and her parents are acting strange. Everyone is struggling, learning and changing together. Everyone must accept the uncertainty that the future brings.

Continuous Challenge and Change

In her book *The Plateauing Trap*, Judith Bardwick examines the learning curve. She says that in the first three months of a new job, employees are inexperienced. They really don't know what they're doing and have to ask a lot of questions. The next 18 months are characterized by rapid learning, in which they are also acquiring new skills. After two years, they reach a plateau where they become "expert."

Research shows that challenge and growth are the primary motivators. How can we keep people continuously challenged in their work?

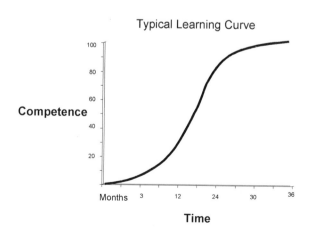

Typical Learning Curve

According to psychologist Abraham Maslow, the greatest human need is to achieve self-actualization, a state in which we blossom, realizing our full potential.[18]

Learning Russian

Harvey Mackay, author of *Swim with the Sharks*, was talking at a conference about learning to speak Russian. Apparently, it takes 400 hours on average for an English-speaking person to learn Russian.[19]

After Harvey's talk, I began to think about what it would really be like to learn Russian in a 40-hour-a-week immersion course. In the first week, nothing would make any sense. Try, try, try and nothing makes any sense. It's all Russian to me. One word sounds exactly like the next. Every time I take a drink of coffee, the instructor says the same thing. I guess she means "cup." After 40 hours in the first week I have learned only "cup," and a few other words! Big deal! In the second week, every time I take a drink the instructor says a different word. I get the impression she means the verb to drink. I learn how to conjugate drink (I drink, you drink, we drink). I learn some other words such as "beer," "another," "please," "washroom." So while I have learned some important things, I would hardly say that I speak Russian. The experience is still characterized by frustration, like writing my name with the other hand.

The first two weeks are characterized by pain. I feel like a failure for 80 consecutive hours. And the pain, fear and frustration wouldn't stop at two weeks. It would continue for months. And then I only gain a little understanding here, have a little "Aha!" over there, but I can't understand the language. So we can plot the experience:

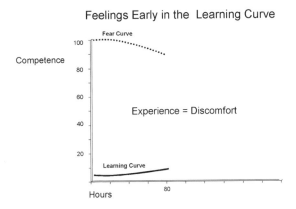

Feelings Early in the Learning Curve

I'm still in the dark. But at some point around 400 hours everything clicks into place. There is a profound "Aha!" And things begin to makes sense. It's like a join-the-dots picture where not all the dots are joined yet, but I can see the whole picture. I even understand words that I have never heard because I can figure out what they mean from the context of the sentence. I can now say with confidence that I speak Russian. All the grammar, all the rules of construction, all the principles of the language and how to speak it make sense. I experience the YES! that kids get when they master a video game. We can plot the experience:

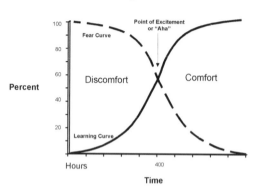

Learning and Fear Curves

As I approach that magical point of 400 hours my frustration, fear and anxiety have been decreasing weekly while I have been learning scattered bits of Russian. But at some point, and it is different for every person, I get the Aha! experience. I have a sense of mastery and control.

As adults we tend not to tolerate the frustration and anxiety of learning new skills. We don't have the patience required to persevere without gratification.

A child taking a first tentative step wobbles and falls over. If it takes 900 falls before the child learns balance, were the 900 scraped knees failures or necessary steps in learning the delicate art of balance?

This is how life works. Life is like a video game. There are rulebooks, such as the wisdom literature of the world's religions, but like kids with the video games, few people read the instructions first. We go through life and we make mistakes. We are doomed to make the same mistakes over and over again until we learn the underlying principles. If we learn the principles, we graduate to the next level and assume more responsibility in life.

We make new mistakes because we face a higher order of challenges. Are the mistakes failures? No! Were the child's scraped knees a failure? Only by giving up the game do we stop learning.

Thus courage and tenacity are characteristics of leadership. Children will naturally continue struggling to learn to walk because the drive is innate. But adults do not naturally struggle to learn new skills. As adults we must be proactive. Only continuous effort brings success. Adults need to develop the "no fear" attitude that children show in learning to walk.

Mackay noted that most of his fellow students quit Russian class after two weeks because they didn't get it. Really, however, they had just not got it "yet." Most people learning a difficult language like Russian quit. And they can honestly say, "I tried my best. I gave it my all for two weeks of intensive study, and I still can't speak or understand Russian." We significantly underestimate the amount of time and effort required to change.

At the end of one presentation, a successful executive came up to me and said, "I have just taken a French course and you are missing the confidence curve."

"The confidence curve?" I asked. "What is it? Help me understand."

"It is what happens to your confidence in this process,"

he replied. "When I started the course, I was very confident. After a couple of weeks of not getting it, my confidence plummeted. I wanted to quit. But I hung in there. As soon as I had the Aha!, my confidence shot up again." Salespeople call this plummet "Death Valley." If new reps can survive Death Valley in their first few months they usually will be good in sales.

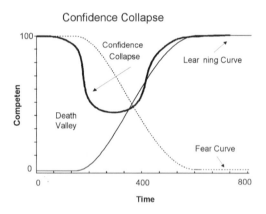

How far would learners' confidence fall while learning subsequent languages? In learning a third language – Spanish, French or Italian – confidence would remain high longer, and when it did fall, it wouldn't fall as far as it did in learning the second language. Learning a fourth language would be easier because of similarities with the languages already spoken. Any dip in the confidence curve would be later and shallower. By the fifth language, learners would have complete confidence in their abilities. No matter what the language or how difficult, learners know they will succeed. They are now truly secure. They have faith in their abilities to learn. This faith can translate into a general faith in the ability to face challenging new situations and learn the necessary skills to succeed.

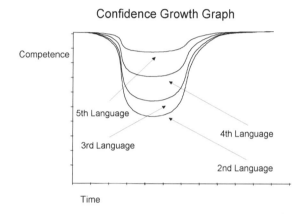

Confidence Growth Graph

Accelerated Learning

The third external presenter at the Achievers Weekend, where the idea for this book emerged, was Blair Singer, a sales trainer.[20] After seeing my presentation Blair asked, "How can we make people more successful, sooner?" What an excellent question! There are three ways to make people more successful sooner: 1) Accelerate learning; 2) reduce fear; 3) increase confidence.

Accelerating learning means making the learning curve steeper. Different people learn different ways. The best way to promote learning is to offer materials that apply to every learning style:

i. *Standardized Training System.* Take an example of a sales organization. Rather than let every new sales rep try to figure everything out on their own through trial and error, successful organizations create a standardized training system that allows a new rep to learn the basics of their job quickly. The system is designed to not overwhelm a new rep – so they learn just enough to be able to start and be successful right away. In other words if the rep is at level one, the training system doesn't teach level 17 information.

ii. *Medium.* Some people prefer to read, others to listen to a tape or a CD and yet others prefer video. So providing training materials in all three formats is important.

iii. *Learning style.* People can be categorized as visuals, auditory or kinesthetic. People who are visual need to "see" either physically or in word pictures to understand a point. Auditory learners need to hear the concepts, while kinesthetic need to have an emotional attachment to deeply understand.

iv. *Personality Type.* People understand information if different ways. There are many courses that teach this such as Myers Briggs, DISC or Wilson Learning Organization's *The Versatile Organization*. *The Versatile Organization* outlines four styles. **Drivers** are fact oriented and want proof, and figures. Drivers want to know how something will impact the bottom line. CEOs typically are drivers. **Expressives** are the visionaries and inventors. *They are excited by the big picture and ideas.* They're not interested in the details. **Amiables** are the people people, the human resource professionals. They make decisions on how they *feel* about something. Finally there are the **Analyticals**, the accountants and engineers of the world who want to know *how* you will do something – they want to know the detailed, step-by-step process. One way to accelerate learning is to ensure that the training material serves the orientation of each type of learner.

These four methods all seek to make the learning curve steeper. In other words shift the learning curve to the left (see graph below).

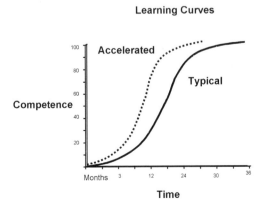

The second way to make people more successful sooner is to reduce their fear. This is what Blair was working on at the Achievers Weekend. Let's take again the example of a new sales rep. If there are typical objections that a new sales rep will encounter, why not prepare him or her to meet these objections in advance? By role playing how to deal with objections, Blair's Sales Dogs training reduces new sales people's fear, increasing their chance of early success. This decreases the fear curve (see graph below).

Fear Curves

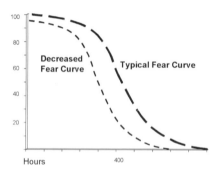

The effect of accelerating the learning curve and decreasing the fear curve is to shift the "Aha" point to the right – the point where the individual feels that they have "got it." By helping sales people be successful earlier an organization can ensure all sorts of benefits – higher sales, increased sales commissions for new reps, lower turn over in sales reps, increased customer satisfaction and greater profitability just to name a few.

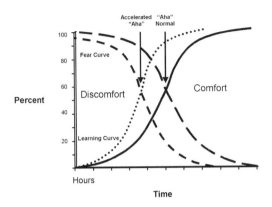

The result of shifting the Aha to the left is to increase confidence. When new sales reps successful sooner their confidence will be higher, and they will be able and willing to take on larger challenges – such as moving to larger and more complex sales sooner. This in turn has a positive impact on the organization's bottom line.

Flow

In Flow: *The Psychology of Optimal Experience,* Mihaly Csikszentmihalyi describes the conditions required to achieve optimal performance. He coined the term "flow."

When you are in flow you lose track of time. The activity you're engaged in takes your full and intense focus, you feel challenged, but not overwhelmed. You have the same feeling as a kid playing a video game. The activity is fun and you take pride in your accomplishments.

In simple terms: if you have a competence equal to 100

> *A man's reach should exceed his grasp, otherwise what's heaven for?*
>
> **Robert Browning**

and are given a job that only requires a skill level of 80 or even 100, you'll be bored because you know how to do it. On the other hand, if you're given a job that requires a skill level of 200 and you'll likely be paralyzed with fear. But with a task at a 120 level you'll be excited and challenged.

Productivity is higher when you're in flow. Obstacles are seen as a challenge – as kids see obstacles in the video game. So it is important to understand flow and the conditions required to achieve it.

Back to the example of a new sales rep, if the organization can accelerate his/her learning helping him/her be successful sooner – the new rep will get into flow faster, be more productive, and enjoy their work.

Learning Continuum

There is a continuum of awareness and learning. We all begin as unconscious incompetents – in other words we don't know what we don't know. A baby doesn't know how to tie its' shoe laces. And it doesn't know that it doesn't know. At some point in time the child will become aware that he doesn't know – he will have moved to the second stage – conscious incompetence. This is a significant improvement over the first stage because now we have a choice to do something about it. We can learn.

Unconscious competence is that we have remained unaware but through circumstance, trial and error, we have improved until we have achieved a certain level of competence. We are good at something – say sales – but we can't tell you why. We are competent but unconscious of the reasons why. We can't critique ourselves. There is no benchmark against which we can measure ourselves.

Finally, there is conscious competence. In this stage we are competent, we know why we are competent, we are continuously measuring ourselves and seeking ways to improve.

In this sense the continuum is circular. The greater my conscious competence, the more I realize that I am an unconscious incompetent. In other words, the more I know, the more I realize there is more to know. Albert Einstein said "We shall always know more, but we will never know everything."

This reminds me of a diver. There are four stages of learning in diving: at the first stage the diver doesn't know anything and relies on the coach to tell him what they did right and wrong. As his skill improves, he comes to guess what he did right or wrong and consult with the coach. At the third stage he knows what he did right or wrong and he no longer needs to consult with the coach. At this point the coach's role changes from telling to exploring ways to improve. The coach moves from telling to mentoring. In the final stage the diver has identified the warning signals of when something is about to go wrong and prevents it before it happens. Now the diver has become self-reflective and self-correcting. There is still a value to the coach, as the coach becomes a research assistant helping the diver explore what new dives are possible. Diver and coach are now equals, both venturing into the future to create new dives.

Human Potential: What Are People Capable of?

What are people capable of achieving? Outside of work, we raise families, negotiate $250,000 mortgages, decide which car to buy from a dozen competing makes, travel all over the world, deal with complex relationships and pursue many interests. But some organizations don't give employees the authority to buy $1.19 worth of paper clips. Even if executives decided to double the spending limit, announcing to employees, "You are now all empowered to go spend $2.38 any way you want to!" The company still would not be tapping the full potential of employees. Few organizations do.

Do you think you have more potential than you realize? Do the people who work for you have more potential than they realize? Your challenge is to help people see what they can't see themselves.

Royal Jelly & The Queen Bee

Nature is fascinating. For the honey bee, or *Apis Mellifera*, life revolves around the Queen Bee.

Pre-eminent in the hive's hierarchy, the Queen Bee is up to 60 percent larger than worker bees, and can live up to 40 times longer, (six years compared to six weeks). She lays an average of 2,000 eggs a day, about two-and-a-half times her own body weight, and spawns more than 5,000,000 bees during the course of her lifetime.

Both the Queen and worker bees are identical at birth, however, their anatomy and physiology become radically different over a period of days. Worker bees are fed a dilute solution of honey, pollen, and nectar, whereas the larvae in the larger Queen cells are continuously fed royal jelly throughout their lives. Any interruption in the diet would halt the transformation of the larvae into a Queen Bee.

Royal Jelly is a creamy-white nutritional substance secreted by the hypo-pharyngeal glands of worker bees. Reserved exclusively for the Queen Bee, royal jelly is the source of her superior attributes.

When a hive becomes too crowded, the Queen will leave with some of the workers to establish a new hive. The workers in the old hive begin feeding royal jelly to up to six fertilized eggs. The first Queen Bee to emerge from her cell will sting the other five developing Queen Bees to death in their cells. If two Queens hatch at the same time, they fight until one dies, as there can be only one Queen in the hive. When a Queen Bee dies the same procedure will occur.

Tibetan Buddhists believe in reincarnation, and that when the Dalai Lama dies, his soul is reincarnated within two years, as a newborn child. After the Dalai Lama dies, monks meditate hoping to receive signs as to where the Dalai Lama's spirit will be re-born.

The current Dalai Lama was found after a series of dreams and visions led senior Lamas to a home in the northeastern province of Tibet. Asking the owners of the house for shelter for the evening, the group leader, Kewtsang Rinpoche, posing as a servant spent much of the evening observing and playing with the youngest child. The child called him "Sera lama." Sera was Kewtsang Rinpoche's monastery. In a few days the group returned, bringing items that belonged to the thirteenth Dalai Lama and items that did not. In every case, the child correctly identified items belonging to the thirteenth Dalai Lama, saying, "It's mine, it's mine." This convinced the search party they had found the new incarnation.

The parents, also convinced of the reincarnation, turned three-year-old Lhamo Thondup over to the Buddhist monks to raise as the fourteenth Dalai Lama. He was taught by the best Tibetan Buddhist teachers, and in an environment of unconditional love. In other words, he was fed a type of royal jelly.

While average individuals in society are not privy to such a rich learning environment, nonetheless incredible spiritual leaders such as Martin Luther King Jr., Mahatma Ghandi, Buddha and mystics such as Meister Eckhart, or poets such as Rumi emerge. I believe we all have the potential to develop far beyond what we perceive our capacities to be, but to do so requires us to put ourselves in a rich learning environment; one that would lead to exceptional and accelerated spiritual growth.

Certain conditions are required for this to occur. First, we must acquire a deep desire and willingness to learn. This implies a sense of awe, wonder and curiosity, or to use a Zen expression, a learner's mind. Secondly, we need to be self-aware, self-reflecting and self-correcting.

Uncovering

While there can only be one Queen Bee in the hive at a time, there can be many spiritually developed people on earth at the same time. Spiritually developed people revel and celebrate the development of others. Spirituality is not limited, it's infinite. Einstein's brilliance in no way detracted from Michelangelo's and Michelangelo's in no way diminished Einstein's. Competitive spirituality is an oxymoron.

Michelangelo's unfinished carvings are breathtaking to look at. In *Atlas the Slave* a perfect torso of a man is emerging from the uncarved bottom of a block of marble, as if he is struggling to get free. Michelangelo said that before he began carving any piece he envisioned the figure he wanted to carve out of the marble block in every detail. His job was to uncover what he already saw inside the piece.

It seems to me that we are all the same. We are born with certain talents, and our job in life is to uncover them. I believe we have no idea of what our real potential is. To find our purpose, what our mission in life is, I believe we should follow Joseph Campbell's advice: "Follow your bliss."

All of these stories (Finding Our True Selves, Royal Jelly & The Queen Bee, Uncovering) raise the question, "How do we evoke or draw out the best in people?"

One day when the subject of leadership was brought up by one of his staff, President Eisenhower took a small piece of string and laid it on his desk.

'Look,' he said. 'If I try to push it I don't get anywhere. But if I pull it, I can take it anywhere I want.'[21]

In the same way leaders need to evoke the best out of people in organizations, communities need to evoke the best out of each other. I must work to evoke the best out of my spouse, and she out of me.

The Rabbi's Story

In the Prologue to *The Different Drum*, M. Scott Peck tells this story. I find it powerful portrait of how we can help each other reach our full potential:

> There is a story, perhaps a myth. Typical of mythic stories, it has many versions. Also typical, the source of the version I am about to tell is obscure. I cannot remember whether I heard it or read it, or where or when. Furthermore, I do not even know the distortions I myself have made in it. All I know for certain is that this version came to me with a title. It is called, "The Rabbi's Gift."
>
> The story concerns a monastery that had fallen upon hard times. Once a great order, as a result of waves of anti monastic persecution in the seventeenth and eighteenth centuries and the rise of secularism in the nineteenth, all its branch houses were

lost and it had become decimated to the extent that there were only five monks left in the decaying mother house: the abbot and four others, all over seventy in age. Clearly it was a dying order.

In the deep woods surrounding the monastery, there was a little hut that a rabbi from a nearby town occasionally used for a hermitage. Through their many years of prayer and contemplation, the old monks had become a bit psychic, so they could always sense when the rabbi was in his hermitage.

"The rabbi is in the woods, the rabbi is in the woods again," they would whisper to each other. As he agonized over the imminent death of his order, it occurred to the abbot at one such time to visit the hermitage and ask the rabbi if by some possible chance he could offer any advice that might save the monastery.

The rabbi welcomed the abbot at his hut. But when the abbot explained the purpose of his visit, the rabbi could only commiserate with him. "I know how it is," he exclaimed. "The spirit has gone out of the people. It is the same in my town. Almost no one comes to the synagogue anymore." So the old abbot and the old rabbi wept together. They read parts of the Torah and quietly spoke of deep things. The time came when the abbot had to leave. They embraced each other. "It has been a wonderful thing that we should meet after all these years, the abbot said, "but I have still failed in my purpose for coming here. Is there nothing you can tell me, no piece of advice you can give me that would help me save my dying order?"

"No, I am sorry," the rabbi responded. "I have no advice to give. The only thing I can tell you is that the Messiah is one of you."

When the abbot returned to the monastery his fellow monks gathered around him to ask, "Well, what did the rabbi say?"

"He couldn't help," the abbot answered. "We just wept and read the Torah together. The only thing he did say, just as I was leaving – it was something cryptic – was that the Messiah is one of us. I don't know what he meant."

In the days and weeks and months that followed, the old monks pondered this and wondered whether there was any possible significance to the rabbi's words. The Messiah is one of us? Could he possibly have meant one of us monks here at the monastery? If that's the case, which one? Do you suppose he meant the abbot? Yes, if he meant anyone, he probably meant Father Abbot. He has been our leader for more than a generation. On the other hand, he might have meant Brother Thomas. Certainly Brother Thomas is a holy man. Everyone knows that Thomas is a man of light. Certainly he could not have meant Brother Elred! Elred gets crotchety at times. But come to think of it, even though he is a thorn in people's sides, when you look back on it, Elred is virtually always right. Often very right. Maybe the rabbi did mean Brother Elred. But surely not Brother Philip. Philip is so passive, a real nobody. But then, almost mysteriously, he had a gift for somehow always being there when you need him. He just magically appears by your side. Maybe Phillip is the Messiah. Of course the rabbi didn't mean me. He couldn't possibly have meant me. I'm just an ordinary person. Yet supposing he did? Suppose I am the Messiah? O God, not me. I couldn't be that much for You, could I?

As they contemplated in this manner, the old monks began to treat each other with extraordinary respect on the off chance that one among them might be the Messiah. And on the off chance that each monk himself might be the Messiah, they began to treat themselves with extraordinary respect.

Because the forest in which it was situated was beautiful, it so happened that people still occasionally came to visit the monastery to picnic on its tiny lawn, to wander along some of its paths, even now and then to go into the dilapidated chapel to meditate. As they did so, without even being conscious of it, they sensed this aura of extraordinary respect that now began to surround the five old monks and seemed to radiate out from them and permeate the atmosphere of the place. There was something strangely attractive, even compelling, about it. Hardly knowing why, they began to come back to the monastery more frequently to picnic, to play, and to pray. They began to bring their friends to show them this special place, and their friends brought their friends.

Then it happened that some of the younger men who came to visit the monastery started to talk more and more with the old monks. After a while, one asked if he could join the order. Then another. And another. So within a few years, the monastery had once again become a thriving order and thanks to the rabbi's visit, a vibrant center of light and spirituality in the realm.

The Head, the Hand, the Heart

True knowledge involves the head, the hand and the heart. Creating change either in myself or within an organization involves working at all three levels. Everywhere I go, people talk about the need to change. Clearly, people know that they have to change (head knowledge). However, many fear change (heart). They dislike the feelings of fear, frustration and inadequacy that they experience when learning. Their fear may be so strong that it paralyzes them, preventing them from taking action (hand). Head knowledge is the *why* to do, hand knowledge the *what* to do, and heart knowledge the *want* to do.

Many people believe that if they just had more knowledge (head) they would be able to change (hand). I fall into that category; I'm a book junkie. I read a book a week and am always looking for the secret, the key, to happiness, joy and success.

> *We are more likely to act our way into feeling than feel our way into acting*
>
> **William James, psychologist**

But I've never been able to read my way into physical fitness. Now I've tried a few times. And I've been sincere in my efforts.

I don't mean to disparage head knowledge – changes in thinking can lead to new behavior. But I could be the worldwide expert on inner ear balance, have written the definitive book on the subject, even teach a course at Harvard, but if I don't know how to ride a bike, knowledge doesn't help. Knowledge is nice but it is *insufficient.*

In fact, head knowledge may not even be necessary. For instance, a seven-year-old kid likely knows nothing about the theory of inner ear balance but it won't prevent him from riding a bike.

Wisdom & Action Are More Important than Knowledge

To know and not to do is not to know. Wisdom involves the application of knowledge, and in this sense it is of a higher order.

Summary

I like to view life as a game. If we really believed that life was a game – how would it change our outlook on life and our behavior? What would we do differently if we knew that we couldn't "fail" – because we began to see setbacks as part of the learning process?

Whenever I am in a hall with a tall ceiling, I ask the audience, "Imagine a pillar stretching from the floor to the ceiling that represents all knowledge in the universe. Both knowledge that we have uncovered as a human race and knowledge we have yet to discover. Where would all collective human knowledge fall as a percentage of all knowledge, close to the top, bottom or middle of the pillar?" Inevitably people respond, "Close to the bottom."

"Okay, let's take all human knowledge, that little section close to the bottom and stretch it out until it represents a pillar from floor to ceiling. Where would my knowledge or your knowledge as an individual fall as a percentage of all human knowledge, close to the top, bottom or middle?" Most people answer, "Close to the bottom."

I only know a tiny fraction of a tiny fraction. Am I not, therefore, a child of the universe? Won't I be scraping my knee all my life? I need to have the same compassion for myself as I would for a child learning to walk.

Chapter Three

Leadership

The Gardener

Many people think of gardening as a passive activity. In fact, it is very active. Do nothing and watch what happens to your garden. Within weeks it'll be over run with weeds. Where there is no gardener, there is no garden.

A gardener has to weed, prepare the soil, plant the seeds, ensure there is enough water and fertilize. But in another sense, the gardener does nothing. The plants grow themselves. It's like a Zen paradox. The gardener isn't completely responsible for the outcome, but without the gardener nothing will happen. It is the same with leadership.

A leader has to create systems and structures within an organization to weed, plant, water, and fertilize on an ongoing basis.

Within an organization gardening involves identifying and removing bad management practices and behaviors. When identified, what corrective action does the organization take?

Which grows faster, flowers or weeds?

In this analogy, planting would equate to hiring the best people with the highest potential possible. What is the organization's hiring strategy? Is it designed to recruit the best and brightest?

Watering. Without frequent water, most plants will die. Is the company meeting all the basic needs of its employees in growing and achieving maximum productivity?

Someone I know went on holidays for six weeks. Before she left she weeded all her garden, but only had time to plant her favorite flowers on one half of the garden. When she returned six weeks later, the half of the garden that had been weeded but had no flowers planted, was again overrun with weeds. By contrast, the other half had weeds but they were very small because they had to compete with the flowers she had planted.

This provides an interesting insight. It is not enough to weed out bad practices in an organization. They must be replaced with good practices. It also highlights that weeding is not a one-time, but an ongoing process.

Self-Leadership

This metaphor of gardening as leadership applies not only to leading other people, but leading myself. If I leave my mind on its own, it will be overrun by weeds, thoughts of anger, resentment, hatred, envy, and jealousy. However, if I want to live a happy, joyous life, it requires active work. I have to actively plant good thoughts. And I have to have a system, a discipline of weeding. I can't just say, "I don't feel like weeding so I won't." I have to engage in the activity of weeding.

This applies to self-leadership as well. On the personal level, weeding involves identifying and removing bad habits. What feedback mechanisms do I have around me? Are people willing to confront me or do I tend to shoot the messenger? Do I help to make people more comfortable when they are confronting me or am I defensive? Do I model the behavior of being open to challenge?

One of the surprising facts from J.P.'s presentation on *Emotional Intelligence* is that most of our daily thoughts are negative. Weeding in this instance involves removing these thoughts and planting positive ones in their place.

What is Leadership? What Motivates Leaders?

There's a powerful exercise that I do with seminar participants that was taught to me by Larry Wilson,[22] the founder of Wilson Learning, and the co-author of *The One Minute Sales Person*.

I ask seminar participants, "Why do you think most people want to be a leader? If you stopped people in the street and asked, 'What are the benefits of being a leader?' What would they say?"

Answers typically include: power, money, executive perks, first class travel, having the resources of the organization at your disposal, control, prestige, recognition, having others listen to you, being able to enact your vision, being able to set direction for the organization, being your own boss.

All these answers come down to power, control, and "being served:"

1. **Power** is the most popular answer. Power can be associated with great wealth or rank, but usually it starts with superiority: being in the position of having the "right and only" answers to most of life's pressing challenges.

2. **Control** involves getting others to follow your direction and includes deploying financial and human resources, and to carry out whatever project, direction or vision the leader decides.

3. **Being Served** includes status, recognition, pay and perks.

Then I ask participants to remember a time when they had the most "magical" experience with a leader. It could be in a business situation, their family, community or church. Thinking about the experience, what made it so magical?

Answers vary: "they took time to listen to my ideas." "They believed I could accomplish a difficult task and mentored me." "They had faith." "They helped me to see the bigger picture." "They shared the credit with me." "He/she saw something in me – some potential, talent or inner power, that I hadn't seen in myself." "She helped me discover something I hadn't yet recognized about myself, it was a huge "aha".

In summary what people describe is how:

1. The leader helped them find their own power, talents and uniqueness. "The leader's role wasn't getting power but giving power –

empowering me."

2. People saw themselves stuck in a rut. They couldn't see a way out. The leader helped them see options and possibilities they hadn't thought of. "Instead of controlling, it was the exact opposite – the leader's role was to set me free."

3. Serving. Magical leadership involved being there to serve. "They helped me remove barriers; they spent time with me to coach me. They believed in me. The sum total of all of this is that they cared, they were there for me, they served me."

In fact the qualities of magical leadership come from what Wilson calls "our true self." Notice how they are 180-degree opposites of what people think are the benefits of leadership.

The true nature of leadership is to help other people find their inner power and potential, then help set them free from limitations that are holding that power back and then help them rediscover their true self. In summary, to help them learn, grow, and develop.

Too often we collectively think that the benefits of leadership are getting power, being in control and having others serve us. But from our own stories – describing the best experiences with leaders in our own lives, we experience the very opposite.

This highlights the concept of "servant leadership," made

popular by the late Robert Greenleaf. This is the kind of leader we follow because we want to.

I was working with the UK cabinet office in their top management program (TMP), which brings together the most senior civil servants in the country for a multi week training and development program. One of the most senior civil servants in the UK has written an essay on leadership where he talks about the leader being "a sin eater." This strikes a powerful chord with me.

The Buddhists have a meditation exercise where they breathe in the anger, fear, frustration and resentment of the world and breathe out love, peace, joy and serenity. It occurred to me that this is what the leader does – breathe in the negative emotions that people have within the organization and breathe out the opposite. *Emotional Intelligence* teaches that to do this requires a high EQ level and *The Learning Paradox* teaches that leaders have to engage in activities that make them uncomfortable.

The Challenge of Leadership

People often envy leaders. I was speaking with a group of 200 managers from a large national bank once. They were complaining about all the problems they faced, including how unresponsive the organization was to their needs. So I asked them, "The higher you rise in an organization, do more or fewer people bring you problems? Are the problems harder or easier to deal with? Does the weight of responsibility grow or diminish? Are the timelines for implementing solutions longer or shorter? Are the consequences of decisions more, or less difficult to anticipate? Are the factors affecting the decisions more, or less numerous? Are the solutions more, or less complex? Do the problems require deeper or simpler analysis? In working with people who bring you problems, do you require more, or less patience? So the higher you go does it require more or less patience, tolerance and compassion?" A woman yelled out, "in theory or in practice?"

> *Example is not the best way to teach it is the only way to teach.*
>
> **Albert Schweitzer, theologian**

The higher you rise in an organization, the greater your tolerance for challenge, pain and complexity must be and the greater your willingness has to be to embrace the learning paradox. The higher you go, the greater the weight you carry; therefore, the deeper your analytical abilities and the greater your patience and perseverance must be. And yet many people equate leadership with perks and prestige. Remember, the higher you go, the thinner the air gets. So at the end of this line of questioning to the group of 200 managers I said, "Remember, you choose to be leaders."

Law of Leverage

Leaders in an organization or entrepreneurs running their own business need to apply what I call the law of leverage.

In theory an individual works 40 hours a week, 50 weeks a year, or 2,000 hours a year. If you run your own business and have sales of $500,000 a year, divide by 2,000 hours you get $250 an hour. So you have to generate sales of $250 every hour that you work and this is based on last year's results, so it doesn't take into account any growth. If you want to achieve 10 percent growth this year, you'll have to earn $275 every hour.

You'll then need to evaluate every single activity as to whether it will yield $275 of top line revenue. If not, you'll have to stop doing it, either by delegating it, or eliminating it through work redesign.

Another way of looking at the same situation is asking, "What alone can I do?" In my case I ask, "Can my assistant write my next book?" No. "Can my assistant book my travel?" Yes. "Can my assistant work out at the gym on my behalf?" No. "Can the office manager negotiate with suppliers?" Yes.

I use the Law of Leverage and ask the question, "What alone can I do?" to help me stay disciplined and focused on what is most important and where I can add the most value.

Sales Time

Here's a staggering fact: sales reps only spend 23 percent of their time selling! Extensive studies by Pace Productivity[23] show that an average sales rep works 46 hours a week, but spends only 10 hours a week selling. By contrast, an average sales rep spends almost half of their time on administration (22 percent), order processing (14 percent) and service (13 percent)! An average sales rep is spending almost 23 hours a week in these three activities!

Sales Reps Time

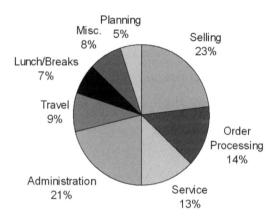

Very small changes in behavior can have significant financial impact. If the organization can eliminate three hours of paperwork a week from these activities – it would give the sales representative three hours more selling time – about 30 percent more time! This would yield 30 percent more sales and 30 percent more commissions for the sales reps and 30 percent more profit for the organization! In other words, a very small change in behavior – changing three hours of activity out of a 46-hour workweek – or a 6.5 percent change in time allocation – yields a 30 percent increase in profitability!

This is why it is so important to eliminate non-value added activities.

FedEx

Today FedEx won't have to answer 700,000 calls because customers are self-serving on the Web – tracking packages, making payment queries, changing information, and paying for shipments. In fact, customers answer twice as many queries themselves using the Web, as they do by calling FedEx. The company hasn't had to hire an additional 20,000 staff as package volumes have grown, and last year FedEx didn't have to pay to print two billion forms, which it would have had to courier out to customers.

Call Deflection

"Call deflection" is when a company diverts a customer inquiry that would have gone to a call center to the Web. Each deflected call has a tremendous financial impact. An average call center interaction will cost a company $32.74. To resolve the issue by e-mail costs $9.99, but if the customer can self-serve and solve the problem over the Web it will only cost $1.17.[24]

This explains why companies such as Dell and Cisco have invested so heavily to make their Web sites so easy to use. Customers will solve their own problems. At Dell, 50 percent of its sales and 70 percent of support is done over the Web. For Cisco, the figures are even higher: more than 90 percent of orders and support is done over the Web.

Homeostasis

Homeostasis is the tendency of a system to stay constant. For instance, the room you're in probably has a thermostat. When the room gets too cold, the heating comes on. When the room gets too hot, the air conditioning comes on. The system works to maintain a constant temperature.

I believe that my sense of self-esteem, (self-worth or a sense of what I deserve) works on the principle of homeostasis. My self-esteem, or sense of self worth, is something that exists both consciously and unconsciously. It's an average of all the good and bad things that I have done in my life – like some accounting ledger.

If things in my life aren't going well, I put my nose to the grindstone and work harder to change the situation, because I know I deserve better. But when things go better than ever before – at some deep level I might not feel comfortable, because I don't deserve it – and I may "sabotage" the situation. That's like the air conditioning coming on.

How then can I set the thermostat to a higher level? Through service – helping others. In particular I am a fan of anonymous service, service rendered without any expectation of return. Service, especially anonymous service, raises the bar of what I feel I deserve. And therefore when good things begin to happen in my life I can happily accept them – because I have raised my sense of self-esteem.

I can't change my self-esteem by thinking – any more than I can change my bank balance through thought. If you disagree, try this: after you have done something that you feel is reprehensible – do affirmations in the mirror: "I am a wonderful human being – an example of light and love in the universe." How did it work? Feel any better?

In other words, it's action that changes my self-perception, not thought or affirmations.

Tithing

The Mormons believe in the concept of tithing. They donate 10 percent of their pre-tax income to charities. I think that this is a wise philosophy.

When my income is modest my tithing is modest. As my income grows so does my tithing. It's a great discipline to get into.

On the west coast of Canada, Aboriginal people measure the greatness of an individual not by what he has, but by what he has given in his life! What a powerful concept.

Think back to envisioning your eulogies – what will have a profound impact is not what we have died with – but how we have served others and what we have given – not just financially, but emotionally.

Time & Value

We're all so busy. We are working longer hours than ever before in North America. If you are a baby boomer you have less time than ever before – looking after aging parents as well as raising kids, trying to balance work and home life. The stresses are tremendous.

What is most important to us? We all say our families. I mean nobody on their deathbed ever said they wished they'd spent more time at the office! So we all say our families are most important – how does our family rank with everything else that competes for our time? How we spend our time communicates powerfully what we value. How much time am I spending with my family? Or does work get the best part of me and then am I exhausted when I return home?

Leading Change

Kurt Lewin was a psychologist studying meat consumption during the Second World War. In North America government officials wanted people to eat less red meat so they could send more red meat over to the war front in Europe. Instead, they wanted people to eat more visceral organs – you know things you have every day – such as kidneys, heart, brains, stomach, intestines, feet, ears and liver from cows, pigs, sheep and chickens.

So imagine that you are the manager of the program to

get people to eat more visceral organs. Actual consumption of visceral organs is understandably low (point A, diagram 1) and your target is to increase consumption (point B). So what would you do to achieve your targets? Most seminar participants answer:

- Advertising – patriotism and the war effort
- Get doctors to make benefits statements – eating heart makes you more passionate
- Celebrity endorsements
- Tax red meat and subsidize visceral organs
- Hold seminars for butchers on how to present visceral organs

Lewin called these activities incentives or *driving forces*, as they were designed to change behavior. Only a portion of the goal was achieved (point C).

As the manager of this program, you know that you only get a bonus if you achieve the objective. So what would you do now? Some participants yell out, "lower the goal." Very clever, but you can't. Other answers typically involve more advertising, more health benefit statements, more celebrity endorsements, etc – in fact doubling all efforts. One new driver typically added at this point is rationing – and this is what actually happened during the war. The availability of red meat was limited.

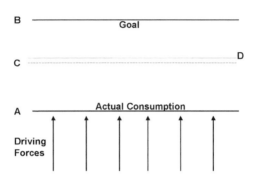

Diagram 1: Driving Forces

The result of doubling all efforts was only a marginal increase in consumption of visceral organs (point D). This led Lewin to hypothesize that there was another set of forces at work. He called these forces barriers to change or *restraining forces*. What would hold you back from consuming visceral organs? Responses typically include:

- Even the thought is gross
- Kids would react badly
- Culture, upbringing, habit
- Look, taste, smell

Do you swap brain recipes with your neighbors? No. So parents don't know how to cook these.

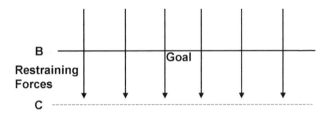

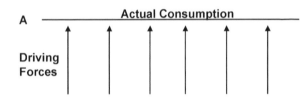

If my car was stuck in the parking lot, I could come into an office and get five guys to come out with me and we would push that sucker – but you know it would be more effective to take the blocks out from under the wheels, take the parking brake off, and take the car out of gear. Whenever we want to create change in an organization, department, or even ourselves, we should first identify the resisting forces and work to reduce or eliminate them before applying driving forces.

But the way most western managers work is to continually apply more drivers and not achieve objectives. In fact, the harder you push with driving forces, the stronger the resisting forces become. What sprang up during the war in response to rationing? The black market. Lewin went on to hypothesize that these restraining forces are like springs. The stronger the force applied to the drivers the greater the resistance. Or in other words, the more you push the more the resistors push back.

The feeling of progress while applying drivers is often illusory. Because once the goal is accomplished – or almost reached, the drivers are removed and applied to some other initiative – and the restraining forces push back.

If you compare the forces, it is interesting to note that the drivers are typically logical. The resistors are typically emotional.

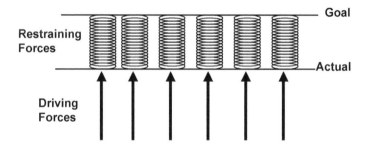

To be successful in a change initiative, an organization must first identify the resistors and develop action plans for each one. Once these resistors are dampened or eliminated, then apply drivers.

Summary

Larry Wilson's exercise in determining the qualities of a magical leader is powerful – and outlines for me how I should act to become a better leader. A leader is not only a "sin eater" motivating those around him by breathing in conflict, anger, fear, and breathing out compassion,

cooperation, tolerance – but someone who actively removes the barriers to help everyone in the organization achieve their full potential.

Final Reflection

It has been a real pleasure to write the book – and I want to leave you with a couple of final reflections.

Tyler

Friends of mine – Wayne or Anne Therese (we call her AT) – have two children: Tyler who is three and Christian who is one. Being parents is a serious responsibility.

The kids get up at 6:30 in the morning and either Wayne or AT get up with them, dress them, play with them, feed them, and then the other parent gets up at 7:30 has a shower, eats breakfast. One parent drops the kids off at day care.

After a long day at work, Wayne or AT picks up Tyler and Christian, takes them home to play with them, feed them, bathe them, and put them to bed. Then Wayne and AT have a short time to themselves and collapse in exhaustion.

Wayne and AT's life revolves around the kids. The work that goes into caring for young children is non-stop, and it's exhausting. In watching Wayne and AT, I begin to appreciate all that my parents have done for me when I never even knew it.

Tyler never says to his parents, "Gee I really appreciate all that you do for me. The non stop work, the worrying about finances and being stressed about my health whenever I am not feeling well. Your whole world revolves around me. You know I never really have stopped to thank you for all this."

It occurred to me that my relationship with God may be

exactly the same as Tyler's and Christian's with their parents. God has provided me with the most wonderful planet in the universe. I was born to wonderful parents who loved me. And they have provided for me their entire lives to the best of their ability. I have three meals a day. I have never known war. I live in the most wonderful country in the world. I have freedom of speech. I can read whatever I want to. Go to movies. And I take all this for granted.

Human Development Taken for Granted

Four million years ago, humans first began walking upright. Two million years ago we began to make tools. Only 35,000 years ago cave paintings appeared. Just 12,000 years ago humans began domesticating plants and animals. Starting only 10,000 years ago most languages and vocabulary were developed. So it took humanity almost four million years to create language. These days most children can speak by the age of two.

The Sumerian language is the oldest written language. It emerged around 3,100 B.C. As written language spread, it was only an elite group that could read and write. It wasn't until the invention of the Guttenberg Press in 1450 – just 550 years ago – that reading and writing became widespread. In Western society we consider reading and writing to be essential skills, and most children have learned these within their first five years. Children today stand on the shoulders of millions of years of human development by the time they are six. And we take it all for granted.

Epilogue

I would very much welcome your comments on *Emotional Learning*. E-mail me at jimh@jimharris.com – and if your suggestions are incorporated in a future edition of the book, I will thank you in the acknowledgements, and send you a complimentary copy of the subsequent edition.

Bibliography

Bandler, Richard & John Grinder. Reframing: *Neuro-Linguistic Programming and the Transformation of Meaning.* Moab, Utah: Real People Press, 1982.

Bardwick, Judith. *Danger in the Comfort Zone.* New York: American Management Association, 1991.
———. *The Plateauing Trap.* New York: Bantam, 1988.

Covey, Stephen. *The 7 Habits of Highly Effective People.* New York: Fireside, 1989.
———. *Principle Centered Leadership.* New York: Summit Books, 1990.
———. *How to Succeed with People.* Salt Lake City: Deseret Book Company, 1971.

Csikszentmihalyi, Mihaly. Flow: *The Psychology of Optimal Experience.* New York: Harper & Row, 1990.

Deming, W. Edwards. *Out of Crisis.* Cambridge, Mass: MIT Center for Advanced Engineering Study, 1982.

Goleman, Daniel, *Emotional Intelligence.* Why it can matter more than IQ. Bantam Books, New York, 1995.

Harris, Jim, *Blindsided!* How to Spot the Next Breakthrough that will Change Your Business. Oxford: Capstone, 2002.

Harris, Jim, *The Learning Paradox.* Oxford: Capstone, 2001.

Kushner, Harold S. *When Bad Things Happen to Good*

People. New York: Avon Books, 1983.

Ornish, Dean. *Dr. Dean Ornish's Program for Reversing Heart Disease*. New York: Ballentine Books, 1991.

Peck, M. Scott, *The Different Drum*. New York: Simon & Schuster, 1987.

Tsai Chih Chung, *Zen Speaks* (translated by Grian Bruya) Anchor Books, Doubleday, New York, 1994.

Acknowledgments

The concept for *Emotional Learning* began at the 2002 Achievers weekend conference for the top 500 business leaders in InterBiz. On Friday night one of the few consultants in North America certified by Daniel Goleman to speak on *Emotional Intelligence*, J.P. Pawliw-Fry, gave a presentation that had a powerful impact on me. After his talk I began to explore how *Emotional Intelligence* related to my second book, *The Learning Paradox*.

My talk began by focusing on the intersection of *Emotional Intelligence* and *The Learning Paradox*. The response to the material was overwhelming.

After the conference, Casey Combden, Rod Schulhauser and I began to explore how we might capture this material in a simple way so that people could receive the benefit – and the idea for this book was born.

So I would like to thank Casey and Rod for their encouragement, J.P. for his awesome presentation at the conference and Daniel Goleman for his fantastic book, *Emotional Intelligence*.

It takes a team of people to produce a book and accompanying materials. I am really excited to be working with Rod Schulhauser of MMTI. I am also grateful to Rod for designing the image for the CD of *The Learning Paradox*. Colin Nanton produced a fantastic *Emotional*

Learning CD audio from the recording of the Collingwood weekend. It's an excellent companion to this book. Colin and I plan to create a second CD audio of *Emotional Learning* by 2003. Michael Cormack edited the initial draft of *Emotional Learning* and Victoria Musgrave the second. Their excellent editing skills greatly improved the text. Kate Anthony designed the cover of the book and CD. I love her simple, clean, powerful design, which to me communicates the story of the Taoist Farmer. I would like to thank Leasa Paquette for her lay out and design of *Emotional Learning*. It was a pleasure to work with her - and I loved how she included the *Emotional Learning* logo in the header of even pages! Finally I want to thank Shawnessy Johnson for updating the Web site to incorporate this new material.

I would like to sincerely thank a number of friends, colleagues and clients who have greatly enriched the text through their insights in reviewing the manuscript: Brian Band, Trish Blake-Jones, Casey Combden, Michael Cormack, Richard Elmes, Jim Estill, Cathy Harris, Shawnessy Johnson, Lee-Anne McAlear, Victoria Musgrave, Catherine Nanton, Rod Schulhauser, Deirdre Sheehan and John Schumacher.

At Strategic Advantage there is a great team of people who have helped work not only on this book, but ensure the smooth operation of the company in the mean time: Lorna Fernandes, Shawnessy Johnson, Mike Cormack and Victoria Musgrave.

Jim Harris

Emotional Learning is Jim Harris' fourth book.

Jim Harris is a one of North America's foremost authors and thinkers on change and leadership. Association magazine ranked him as one of the North America's top ten speakers. As a management consultant Jim speaks internationally at over 40 conferences a year and conducts strategic planning sessions with executive teams, focusing on the most pressing issues:

- Leadership in the New Millennium
- Customer Relationship Management
- eLearning
- IT and Future Trends
- Change, Creativity & Innovation
- Creating Learning Organizations

Mr. Harris also leads workshops on:

- Strategic planning amid complexity
- Creating Common Mission/Vision

Mr. Harris' second book, *The Learning Paradox*, was nominated for the National Business Book Award in Canada, and has appeared on numerous bestseller lists. Books for Business has ranked it as one of the top 10 business books in all of North America. There are now over 40,000 copies in print. *The Learning Paradox* argues that "job security" as we knew it is gone. Individual and organizational security is now based on learning, changing and coping with uncertainty. Paradoxically these are what we as adults fear most!

His third book, *Blindsided!* was released in August 2002 as one of the lead titles for UK based Capstone, part of John Wiley & Sons of New York. *Blindsided!* was published simultaneously in 80 countries worldwide. In October 2001 Polaroid declared bankruptcy. The company that came to define instant photography was blindsided by the rapid rise of digital photography. *Blindsided!* highlights why companies and even whole industries are being blindsided and then answers the questions: How can decision makers identify early warning signs? How can leaders put in place systems and structures that will prevent their organizations from being blindsided? And then knowing all this, how can you blindside your competition?

He also co-authored the national bestseller *The 100 Best Companies to Work for in Canada* – selling 50,000 copies. As a management consultant, Mr. Harris works with leading businesses, *Fortune 500* companies, and organizations aspiring to join these ranks. From 1992-1996 he represented the Covey Leadership Center in Canada – teaching Dr. Stephen Covey's work, *The Seven Habits of Highly Effective People* to clients.

His clients include the Agilent Technologies, Association of Research Libraries, Barclays Bank, Bell Canada, Centra, CIBC, Columbia Tristar Pictures, Connaught Laboratories, Credit Union Executives Society, Certified Managment Accountants, Deloite & Touche, European Snack Food Association, General Motors, Glaxo Wellcome, Hallmark Cards, International Council Shopping Centers, IABC, IEEE, Investors Group, ISOPIA (now Sun Microsystems), JD Edwards, Johnson & Johnson, Lego, Mackenzie Financial, MasterCard, Meeting Professionals International, Munich Re, Novartis, NEC, Nortel Networks, Pasteur Mérieux Connaught, Royal Bank, Royal LePage Commercial Real Estate, RBC Dominion Securities, Saba, Society of Management Accountants, Society of Professional Engineers, Sybase, SHL Systemhouse, Sun Life Assurance, The Executive Committee, TNT Worldwide Express, Unitel, UK Cabinet Office and Zurich.

For more information on booking Jim Harris visit www.jimharris.com.

EndNotes

[1]This story appears in Richard Bandler and John Grinder. *ReFraming*. (Utah: Real People Press, 1982) Page 1.

[2]Daniel Goleman, *Emotional Intelligence*, (New York: Bantam Books, 1995) page 34.

[3]www.ksu.edu/humec/c&t.htm.

[4]Film critic Michael Medved.

[5]www.ksu.edu/humec/c&t.htm

[6]Gary Bauer and Dr. James Dobson, *Children at Risk: The Battle for the Hearts and Minds of Our Kids*. (W Publishing Group, 1994). Similar facts are documented by Kansas State University College of Human Ecology www.ksu.edu/humec/c&t.htm.

[7]I have to thank Ed Foreman a professional speaker for this insight. Ed can be reached at Executive Development Systems, 3818 Vinecrest Dr. Dallas, TX 75229 or call (800) 955-7353. www.edforeman.com.

[8]This comes from *Alcoholics Anonymous*, page 60-61.

[9]Harold S. Kushner. *When Bad Things Happen to Good People* (New York: Avon Books, 1983) page 61-62.

[10]Ibid, page 63.

[11]There are over 1,000 species of bamboo! www.agctr.lsu.edu/Inst/International/pdf/bamboo.pdf

[12]Forrester Research Inc.

[13]Fortune, "Brands Rule," Mar. 4, 1996.

[14]Figure provided by Cott Corporation.

[15]National Center for Educational Statistics. Digest of Educational Statistics, 1999.

[16]Stephen R. Covey, *How to Succeed with People* (Salt Lake City, Utah: Deseret Book Company, , 1971), page 23.

[17]*Information Week 500*. The complete rankings from 1995 to

2000 can be found on their website at
www.informationweek.com.

[18]On his deathbed Maslow actually refuted this claim,
suggesting that the highest need is self-transcendence,
working for some larger, worthier goal than just our own
interests. Paradoxically, the only way an individual can
achieve self fulfillment is through service to others.

[19]National Speakers Association 1995 Convention,
Minneapolis, July 15-18, 1995.

[20]To find out more on Blair Singer visit www.salesdogs.com

[21]General Dwight D. Eisenhower, *Reader's Digest*, May 1957,
p. 27. (Provided by Herb Pankratz at the Eisenhower
Library).

[22]For more information about Larry Wilson, go to
www.larrywilson.com.

[23]"How Sales Reps Spend Their Time" by Mark Ellwood of
Pace Productivity. For more information visit
www.getmoredone.com/research2.html.

[24]James Watson, Gail Donnelly and Joshua Shehab. *The Self-
Service* Index Report Doculabs. First Quarter 2001. Table 2.